PORTLAND NECK:

THE HANGING OF

THOMAS BIRD

by

Jerry Genesio

To my love,

Judy,

whose patience,

understanding,

and support

have made it possible

for me

to pursue

my dreams.

ACKNOWLEDGEMENTS

I wish to acknowledge with the most heartfelt thanks the research assistance provided by Thomas Gaffney, PhD, former Special Collections Librarian in charge of the Portland Room at the Portland Public Library, Portland, Maine.

A special thanks is owed to the staff at the National Archives, Waltham, Massachusetts, for leading me to a thin manila folder containing a handwritten record of the capture and examinations of the surviving crew of the English sloop *Mary* off the coast of Maine, the trial of Hans Hanson and Thomas Bird, and Thomas Bird's execution.

I also want to thank the Interlibrary Loan staff at the Portland Public Library, Portland, Maine, the Bridgton Public Library, Bridgton, Maine, and the New Hanover County Public Library, Wilmington, North Carolina, for helping me find hard copies of many of the reference books I needed to complete this project.

And I must recognize the incredible convenience and invaluable information provided by the Google Books Library Project, which made it possible for me to access many very rare and hard-to-find antiquarian books on the Internet. Without this amazing resource, this account of the sloop *Mary's* adventures on Africa's Guinea Coast would have been very much shorter and thinner.

PROLOGUE

This is an account of the last years of the life, and death, of an Englishman named Thomas Bird who was hanged in Portland, Maine, on June 25, 1790. He was the first person to be executed by a judicial order handed down by our nation's young federal court system created by the Constitution of the United States of America. Surprisingly little has been written about the incident. Several brief articles were published in *The Cumberland Gazette,* Portland's only newspaper at that time; a few short paragraphs appear in various early histories of the city of Portland, of the state of Maine, and of Maine's system of jurisprudence; and a brief article written by the author and published by the Maine Historical Society appeared in *Maine History 42:4 July 2006.*

Bird, but 40 years of age and a mariner from the eighth year of his life, was the only individual held accountable for the "piratical murder" of John Connor, Master of the English sloop *Mary,* though it was known that others were involved before, during, and after the fact. Two of these individuals, a young Norwegian named Hans Hanson, and a seasoned American mariner named Josiah Jackson, were captured with Bird and both were jailed with him in

Portland, though Jackson was held a very short period of time.

History cannot be read as a list, for no worldly event that is in any way related to the human condition occurs in a vacuum. Then, as now, the roles of all actors on the stage of history are created by many circumstances beyond their control that influence their lives and their decisions either consciously or, perhaps more often than not, at a level shrouded well beneath their vista of consciousness. All of those involved in this trial, with the possible exception of Hans Hanson, held vivid memories of a very bitter war between England and her American colonies that was not formally ended until the Treaty of Paris was signed on September 3, 1783, less than seven years earlier.

On October 18, 1775, less than fifteen years before the trial of Bird and Hanson, Portland was burned to the ground by the crews of four Royal British Navy vessels under the command of Captain Henry Mowatt. According to William Willis' *History of Portland*, of the 414 structures destroyed in the conflagration, 136 were homes, and winter was approaching. Donald A. Yerxa, who published a master thesis on the incident, wrote that George Washington referred to the town's destruction as "an Outrage exceeding in Barbarity & Cruelty every hostile Act practiced among civilized Nations."

The rebuilding of Portland was still in progress at the time of the trial. Benjamin Titcomb, whose name appears on a list of personal losses sustained by the inhabitants in the destruction of the town, was foreman of the federal grand jury that indicted Bird for murder, and Hanson for being an accessory to that crime. And Nathaniel Wilson, a member of the committee charged with compiling the list of personal losses, was a member of the federal petit jury that convicted Bird, but acquitted Hanson.

U.S. District Court Judge David Sewall and all officers of the court, excepting only the two defense attorneys, were military officers during the American Revolution. At the time of the trial, three of these held high rank in the Maine militia: Clerk of the Court Henry Sewall, the judge's cousin, was a colonel; U.S. District Attorney William Lithgow, Jr., who was seriously wounded at Saratoga, and U.S. Marshal Henry Dearborn both held the rank of major general. In addition, Cumberland County Sheriff John Waite served as a captain during the war, and held the rank of colonel in the Maine militia during the trial.

Thomas Bird was a man who stood before this court charged with the murder of his master. In light of the fact that there is but one extant facsimile of Bird's signature, which consists only of his "mark", it can be surmised that he was illiterate and understood little of the judicial process that had enveloped him. He had, several times during the American Revolution, been taken prisoner, but had always been eventually exchanged or released unharmed. He thought of America as a place of refuge on several such occasions, signing on with American vessels to avoid the press gangs of the British Royal Navy. But

Thomas Bird now found himself in the hands, and at the mercy, of twelve men who had suffered substantial loss in one way or another during America's war with England, and he was an Englishman.

Shortly after their capture and arrest, Bird, Hanson, and Jackson were each questioned, and these examinations were recorded, which recordings are part of the trial record held at the Federal Archives in Waltham, Massachusetts. But neither Bird, Hanson, nor Jackson put their signature or mark on these documents to corroborate their answers. There is no mention of whether the suspects were questioned together, separately, or even if they were under oath, though with regard to Hanson, written above his statement are the words "In the Court of Admiralty Seated at Portland in the County of Cumberland, 23 July 1789".

Thomas Bird's *Dying Statement* has served as the primary resource for dates and African place names that appear in the record but the author has been unable to verify or confirm. Cartography, in the 18th century, was far from being an exact science, and most maps were drawn exclusively for navigators who shared the cartographer's native language. Though some map makers used Latin for notations and to identify natural features and developed locations, this resulted in merely adding yet another name to every feature and location previously identified by English, Spanish, Dutch, French, Portugeuese, and other explorers who attempted to commit their world to parchment. Further, over the course of 220 years, many of these names have been changed numerous times. Nevertheless, many hours spent studying 18th and 19th century maps and books focusing on Africa's Guinea Coast have made it possible to identify virtually all of the *Mary's* ports of call there with near certainty.

It must also be noted that Thomas Bird, and very likely Hans Hanson as well, were illiterate and had to rely on phonetics when recalling the various African place names that they knew. Josiah Jackson, on the other hand, was both literate and capable of reading navigation charts.

Thomas Wait, editor of the *Cumberland Gazette*, very carefully wrote Bird's *Dying Statement* as it was dictated. Bird's, Hanson's, and Jackson's examinations, however, were transcribed as the subjects were being questioned, presumably under some duress, and very probably by someone other than the person directing the examination. The questions may have been posed by one or more of the judges seated on the court before which the examinations were held, or by some other officer(s) of the court.

The individuals recording their responses to these questions may have had difficulty understanding every word that was spoken and, particularly given the crudeness of the writing tools of that time, very probably had difficulty keeping up with the pace of the procedure. On the record of Hanson's examination, it was noted that one of the transcribers, a Mr. Bradbury, was replaced. The transcriptions of the three examinations also reflect the penmanship of several different hands subject to the understanding and interpretations of several different individuals. Further, Jackson's and Bird's responses were written in the first person perspective, while Hanson's was written in the third person.

Judge Samuel Freeman (1742-1831), who was very likely privy to most, if not all, of the legal discussions and decisions relating to the trial, and who, in 1821, published a collection of historical information about Portland, tells us that Josiah Jackson "was improved as a witness." As there is no record indicating that Jackson was tried for any crime, nor that the federal grand jury handed up any indictment against him, we can assume that he was granted immunity in exchange for testifying against one or both of his crew members.

Aside from the above, the reader should bear in mind that the narrow stretch of land called Portland Neck, which is now occupied by the city of Portland, was part of Falmouth until 1786. Nevertheless, it is referred to herein consistently as Portland, without regard for the occasional anachronism, in the interest of avoiding confusion.

I

THOMAS BIRD

Thomas Bird was born in November of 1749 at Abbots Leigh, a small village on the south bank of the River Avon near the port city of Bristol, then England's second largest city. The parish of Abbots Leigh rested midway between the center of Bristol and the mouth of the Avon, which emptied into the Bristol Channel and, flowing further to the west, mixed with the waters of the Celtic Sea. In his early youth, Thomas may have seen a thousand vessels anchored on the Avon or tied to the docks further upriver at Bristol, their masts giving the river the appearance of a large forest of hardwood trees bare of leaves and gently swaying in the breeze. Sitting on the bank of the river as a child he surely imagined the strange and distant places these ships and their crews had sailed to, the violent storms they had survived, and the treacherous pirates their cannons and cutlasses had vanquished. Such imaginings are the bedrock of every young boy's dreams.[1]

Young Thomas was safely beyond the stench, filth, and squalor of inner Bristol's narrow streets. His parents, George and Ann Bird, were of some means for when he was eight years of age they sent him off to school, which was well beyond the resources of the poor. But he'd been so captivated by the lore of maritime adventure that he immediately ran away and, in the company of his uncle, he went off to sea. After a single voyage, young Thomas was apprenticed to a Captain John Smith of Bristol, whom he served for the next seven years. At about the age of 17, having completed his apprenticeship, he struck off on his own serving masters engaged in the slave trade where, sailing between Africa and the West Indies on one ship or another, he hung his hammock for the next decade of his life, until England's war with her American colonies.

At the very outset of America's revolution, about the time that British Captain Henry Mowatt ordered the destruction of Portland, Maine, the vessel that Thomas Bird served on was captured by a privateer out of Marblehead, Massachusetts. He was taken prisoner, carried eventually to Boston, and finally New York, where he was exchanged. Returning to Bristol he frequented the docks in search of work, fell into the hands of a Royal Navy press gang, and was forced to serve on board the *HMS Medea*, a British frigate. Finding service on a British naval war vessel not to his liking, he deserted 10 months later at Hull and traveled to Liverpool where he shipped out aboard the brig *Edward*, commanded by a Captain Parks, which was bound for New York. The *Edward* was captured by the brig *General Glover*, and he was once again taken to Marblehead.

Whether he was released or pressed into service by the Americans, he sailed out of Marblehead and Salem for the next three to four years until, near the end of the war, the American privateer *Eagle* on which he was serving was taken by the *HMS Hind* and the *HMS Wolfe*, and he was carried to Quebec, Canada. Three weeks later he shipped aboard a brig bound for Scotland. In the month following his arrival, he signed on with a Captain Rankin and boarded the *Ruby*, which was bound for New York. There he fell afoul of another English press gang and was placed on board the *HMS Vulcan*, but once again deserted at Sandy Hook on the New Jersey coast and found his way to Philadelphia. In a short time he was taken on board a brig under the command of a Captain Thomas, who was bound for Tenerife in Spain's Canary Islands, but on their arrival the vessel foundered on a rocky reef and was lost.

Bird survived the ordeal and soon sailed from Tenerife aboard a Spanish cutter out of Cadiz on which he remained for nearly a year, finally being discharged in Portugal. He picked up an English frigate at Lisbon, left her at Portsmouth, England, and traveled to Liverpool where he once again signed on with a slave trader bound for Africa. Eventually returning to Liverpool he then joined the crew of the slave trader *Favourite* sailing with her back to Africa, on to the West Indies with a slave cargo, and left her service when she docked at London in December of 1785 or January of 1786.

Haunting the crowded pubs and cold, wet quays of England's port cities for a month, Bird spent his earnings and was searching for another ship to sail with when he was seized, once again, by a British press gang. They led him aboard the *HMS Bombay*, a cruiser of the Royal Navy,[2] which was then lying at Portsmouth. It was his home for nearly two years but finally, in late August or early September of 1787, he was discharged.

Had he chosen to hang about the docks of London, he might have been drawn, or perhaps even pressed, to serve on a vessel then tied up on the north side of the Thames River at Wapping Stairs. She was the *Bethia*, a merchant ship built three years earlier[3] and purchased by the Admiralty for an ill-fated voyage intended to deliver breadfruit trees from Tahiti to the British West Indies where their fruit was to serve as an inexpensive food for slaves. Retrofitting had already begun under the direction of Sir Joseph Banks, a botanist, and Lieutenant William Bligh of the Royal Navy was appointed to command the voyage. The *Bethia* was to be rechristened the *HMS Bounty*, a name familiar to all with an interest in naval

4

history and adventure.[4] If Bird had sailed with the *Bounty*, he might not have fared better. Seventeen of the forty-six on that voyage were dead by October 29, 1792; three of them hanged for mutiny.[5]

There is no record of where Thomas Bird was discharged from the *HMS Bombay*, but within six or seven days, he found himself on board the sloop *Mary*, which was tied up to one of the docks at Plymouth. She was a cutter-rigged affair of about 30 tons burden, and was being outfitted for a voyage to Africa's Guinea Coast under the command of Captain John Connor, who also owned a share of the *Mary*. His partners in the vessel and the venture were Clarke & Hadley, Merchants, of London.[6]

The *Mary* was a Gravesend boat[7], registered in the town of Gravesend about 25 miles east of London on the south bank of the Thames, which was the normal point of departure for London vessels.[8] But for some unknown reason, Connor had chosen to sail from Plymouth. He was engaged in the slave trade and, if he sought to recruit an experienced crew, he knew the home port for nearly all of England's slave ships was Liverpool. Perhaps he sought to escape his reputation, for he also knew the brotherhood of seamen eagerly shared information about the temperaments and tendencies of the masters they served[9], and any who had sailed with John Connor were unlikely to have fond memories of him.[10]

Connor had signed up six men for the voyage and the tasks at hand: Thomas Morgan, First Mate; Hans Hanson, a 17-year-old Norwegian lad; Thomas Bird; Edward Tool; Jacob Blackman; and another known only as Alex.[11] Morgan surely would have been classified at least as an "able seaman", well versed in his trade, but more likely carried the credentials of a first or chief mate. He stood next in command, was responsible for managing the ship's maintenance, cargo, and crew, and had to have a working knowledge of navigation in the event that the captain became incapacitated or died at sea. It is uncertain if there were others among them who also qualified. Bird, with 29 years of experience, was a seasoned seaman well acquainted with the slave trade, but his illiteracy must have presented a major handicap insofar as charts and navigation were concerned. Like the other four common crew members, he was likely classified as an "ordinary seaman".[12]

The *Mary*, being but a sloop, was small enough to allow its master almost constant and complete knowledge of the tiny wooden world that existed within the embrace of its gunwales. She may have been 50 to 60 feet in length, with a 20 to 25 foot beam, and about a 5 to 5½ foot depth of hold. It would not have been necessary for Morgan to have had impeccable credentials and it's very likely that he did not or he'd have been earning more in wages on a much larger vessel. The same may be said of the other crew members.

Few seamen chose to serve on slave traders if they had other options, and for very good reasons. Along the African coast, "(m)alaria, yellow fever, scurvy, and dysentery were common", especially during the hot, summer months.[13] More seamen on slave voyages died of fever and dysentery than any other cause.[14] "Of 1,080 persons sent out to Africa by the Company of Merchants Trading to Africa from 1751 to 1788, 653 died; 333 of these perished during the first year".[15]

It's very possible that Connor had purchased some, or perhaps even all, of his crew members from *crimps* or *spirits*. The former frequented pubs and taverns searching for drunken sailors who could not pay their bill, or who could be robbed to guarantee that predicament. The *crimp* would settle with the barkeep and the victim would be sold at a profit to the captain of a slave ship, often still in a drunken stupor. *Spirits* preyed on the unemployed and desperate whose feet, theretofore, had been firmly planted on *terra firma*. They were promised high wages, an escape from their debts and family responsibilities, and a life of adventure at sea. Very often the *spirit* even provided his victim an advance against future wages, and then, like the *crimp*, would sell his quarry at a handsome profit.[16]

We don't know where Connor outfitted the *Mary* for the voyage, but her hold was heavy with trading goods including knives, brass and pewter pans and kettles, bolts and pieces of India calico and patterned cloth, colored

7

glass beads, and sundry other items that he planned to offer in bartering for gold, ivory, and slaves. The vessel was also carrying several sheets of copper in her belly that Connor had agreed to deliver to Thomas Horman who operated a store or trading post some 50 miles inland beyond the mouth of Africa's Lapongus River.[17] In addition, there were stores of victuals, rum, and gunpowder for Connor and his crew, as well as their meager personal belongings, a dozen or more guns, and at least as many pairs of manacles for restraining human cargo.[18]

Some time before the end of September 1787, the *Mary* set sail. The prevailing winds and currents carried her southward, past Eddystone Rocks, toward Africa's Guinea Coast. Captain John Connor, First Mate Thomas Morgan, Thomas Bird, and Alex would never again rest their eyes on England.

II

The Guinea Coast

John Connor was a gold, ivory and slave trader, but not necessarily in that order. He plied the waters of the Guinea Coast and the Bight of Benin frequently sailing up one or another of western Africa's copious rivers, many of which the sloop *Mary* could navigate, but the larger ships could not. Markets on the banks of these rivers, some of them 100 miles distant from their mouths, traded gold dust and nuggets, elephant's tusks, and slaves to those

Europeans who were daring enough to risk the unpredictable nature of the native tribes, and of the continent's wild and whimsical interior. Many of the slaves were members of rival tribes defeated in battle, others had been abducted from the villages of adversaries, and some had been sentenced to be sold for having committed a crime, or fallen into indebtedness.[19]

Most of the gold and ivory Connor acquired was returned to England where, if the market was not favorable, it could be stashed and held for better times. But the slaves were perishable goods and Connor wanted to be rid of them before they fell sick of some disease, or managed to leap from the boat into the river where, with hands and often feet manacled, they would drown or be eaten by sharks and crocodiles. The *Mary* sailed as quickly as the winds and currents would carry her to the larger slave trading vessels anchored offshore, offering them first to the buyer who had been waiting the longest to fill his hold. This captain, and perhaps more importantly his crew, would be getting very anxious to set sail for the Caribbean, and would be inclined to offer the best price. His vessel may have been anchored for four or five months, or perhaps even longer, and some of the slaves he had purchased in the first weeks following his arrival were quite possibly already dying from disease or the utter loss of hope known as melancholy. They were crammed below deck on wooden racks resembling deep shelves, pressing against one another with only stale and putrid air to breath, ankles bound by shackles and chains that frequently wore through their skin opening festering wounds. Most masters dared not allow them to be unshackled, much less topside for exercise and fresh air, until they had set sail and were well beyond the sight of land, knowing many would leap from the ship at the first opportunity and, because of the shackles or the sharks, meet with certain death.[20]

The *Mary* reached her destination nine weeks after leaving England, in late November or early December of 1787, anchoring off Salos Island* in the vicinity of Cape Lahou, which marks the end of the Ivory Coast to the west, and the beginning of the Gold Coast to the east.[21] Here in the town of Grand Lahou, situated on the west bank of the Lahou River, traders could find gold dust of superior quality, and ivory, both in abundance.[22] The *Tyger*, an English factory ship†, lay nearby and Connor ordered his men to lower the longboat so he could be taken to meet with Captain Thomas Bullen, commander of the vessel and an agent of Bodee's of London, Merchants. Connor was given permission to transfer much of the *Mary's* cargo to the *Tyger* so he would have sufficient room below for transporting the slaves he hoped to acquire. Bullen then advised Connor where he might purchase some slaves and

---

* Believed to be a small island near Cape Lahou now known by another name.
† A slave ship that transported African men, women and children as cargo.

11

three or four days after their arrival they weighed anchor, tacking westward along the African coastline.

Connor, Bird, and perhaps others on the *Mary* had seen the Guinea coastline many times in the past. By the late 18th century Europeans had built 40 forts along the 1,500 miles of hills, cliffs, mangrove swamps and sandy beaches that had, up to that time, already born the footprints of nearly 30 million human beings who had been reclassified as cargo. Fourteen of these forts, or factories as they were called, were English. The remainder were the property of the Dutch, Danes, French, and Portuguese[23], all protected by sturdy barricades, batteries of cannon, and a contingent of each respective country's military. The governor or commander, usually the factor* of a slave trading company, also oversaw a dozen or more clerks, mechanics and junior agents. Within the walls of each fort there were prisons or enclosed holding pens called *barracoons*, which housed the slaves that had been purchased for resale to those who would deliver them to the Americas or the Caribbean islands. But often enough, these governors were unable to supply all of the ships anchored offshore for months at a time, and that was a weakness that John Connor exploited.[24]

The Lahou and several other rivers to the west, including the Cavally and the Sesters, were easily navigable by small vessels like the *Mary*, and the native populations of the

---

* Business agent.

many villages on their banks were peaceful, and numbered in the tens of thousands. The people of the River Sesters produced vast quantities of rice, which slave traders sought to feed their human cargo. The River Cavally, which flows deep and wide for many miles before spilling into the ocean at Cape Palmas on the western edge of the Ivory Coast, was a desirable location for a trading post. A town of the same name on the Cavally was noted for its trade in ivory, grains of paradise*, beads, and red pepper.[25]

Connor sailed the *Mary* some 50 miles up a river that Bird called the Lapongus to Thomas Horman's trading post, where they offloaded the several sheets of copper Horman had ordered, and they remained for about a week. When they left, they returned to Cape Lahou where Connor passed much of his time dining and discussing business with Captain Bullen.

The following week they ascended a different river to a village where they bought rice and a few gold nuggets. There were no slaves to be had there, so they proceeded to a village some distance up yet another river where they remained for about a month laying close to a village called Pocum. Perhaps the chief of the settlement informed Connor that he had sent a party to raid a rival village and expected them to return with prisoners because, when the *Mary* did finally depart, she left with three slaves manacled and chained in the hold below. However, prior

---

* An exotic pepper.

to their departure, Hans Hanson, Jacob Blackman, and Alex fell sick and were taken ashore. Connor arranged for them to be taken to the village of Mumford on the coast when they recovered, and he agreed to meet them there. He then returned to the *Tyger* where he sold the slaves to Captain Bullen.

Connor decided he could do little with half a crew so he sailed to Mumford, anchoring offshore, and remained there for about four months. During this period he spent much of his time ashore and aboard other vessels in the harbor drinking and dining with others who were, in one way or another, engaged in trade. Returning to the *Mary* one night at about 11 o'clock, he found no one on watch and burst into a fit of rage. Picking up the pump brake handle, he struck First Mate Morgan with it more than 20 times, demanding all the while to know why he didn't keep watch. As Morgan lay on the deck badly injured, Connor jumped on his chest, and then went below.

There was little anyone could do to comfort Morgan and the next morning he was still lying where he had fallen. Regaining consciousness Morgan begged for water, but Connor would not permit the men to wet his lips. Later that day Morgan died and Connor ordered Tool to sew the first mate's body into his canvas hammock and throw him overboard. Tool refused and Bird supported him, demanding that Captain Bullen be summoned to witness what had been done. But Connor's response was to take up the pump brake handle again, beating Tool with it and turning to promise Bird more of the same. In that moment, Edward Tool leaped into the harbor and swam for his life, fortunately making it to shore. Now terrified of his master, and having good reason to believe he would follow through on his promise, Bird sewed Morgan's body into his hammock and threw it overboard. It was then about 4 o'clock in the afternoon.

It is uncertain whether any of the three men who had fallen sick at Pocum had yet returned, but it is reasonable to believe they had not as Hanson made no reference to this memorable event during his examination. This premise could also explain Bird's reluctance to challenge Connor further for, if true, there were at that point no other witnesses to Morgan's murder remaining aboard the *Mary*. In further support of this contention, that evening Captain Connor went ashore and returned with two American mulattoes named James and Sam.

Before Connor ordered the men to weigh anchor, Hans Hanson and Jacob Blackman returned, reporting that Alex had died. With five crewmen now on board, Connor purchased a puncheon[*] of rum for the hold, and 16 slaves, which he offered to a Dutch ship's captain, who declined. But the Dutchman warned Connor that there was war in the country[†] and invited him to lay alongside where the

---

[*] A large cask of no specific capacity.

[†] According to Alexander G. *Findlay's Sailing Directory for the Ethiopic or South Atlantic Ocean* published in 1867, the region's Ashantee and Fantee tribes were frequently at war during this period.

Mary might be protected.[26] However, rather than lay about for weeks or longer with 16 slaves below, Connor decided to return to the *Tyger* and transferred all of his cargo, including the slaves, to Captain Bullen's vessel. He then had the *Mary* raised with block and tackle attached to the larger ship, and he put his crew to work cleaning the sloop's hull of barnacles.

Nine or ten of the slaves that Connor had purchased may have appeared sickly, too old, or in some way a risky investment, for Bullen didn't want them either. When the hull cleaning was done and the *Mary* was lowered, Connor sailed some 70 leagues* until he finally sold them to the master of a Danish factory ship.

Ascending the rivers or even approaching the coastal settlements was apparently not yet considered safe for another week or two as Connor spent this time ferrying several seamen between as many vessels. Another man, known only as Jack, who had taken sick with a fever that was perhaps considered contagious and incurable, was according to Bird "put ashore on a desolate island." Connor also hired an Englishman named William Huddy to replace Morgan as first mate, though we are not told which vessel Huddy came from, or if he met Connor ashore after deserting another ship's company.

---

* About 250 miles.

Now, with a full crew of six men once again, Connor sailed for Cape Mount[†], 500 miles to the west and north of Cape Lahou, arriving three weeks later. Cape Mount is aptly named for it is a promontory with cliffs rising over 1,000 feet above the sea. They approached on the west side where a village rested at the mouth of a river and fresh water spilled from the ground beside a large tree.[27]

The captain was sick for several days, but recovered, ordered his crew to replenish the *Mary's* fresh water supply, and purchased ivory from a brig anchored nearby. During the following week Bird said "the molattoes [sic] and myself being abused by the Captain ran away", but they were stopped by local natives who returned them to the *Mary*; very likely a profitable sideline for those who remained observant and recognized the signs and the smell of fear.

Connor put James and Sam in irons and the next day took them to Sinou Bay, more commonly known as Snow Bay, 150 miles to the southeast. Here the Sinou, a small river, intruded upon a long yellow beach to mix its fresh water in the salty bay. Beyond the beach, the lush, verdant canopy of a forest danced invitingly to the rhythm of the ocean breeze.[28] But Captain Connor paid little heed to the beauty of the African coast for he had only business on his rum-soddened mind. He ordered the men to lower his longboat and he took James and Sam to a Dutch factory

---

[†] On the coast of what is now Liberia.

ship anchored close by, where he sold them. The *Mary* made sail for Krou Settra the same day.

Tacking southeasterly along the Krou Coast they first came upon Settra Krou, identified by two large trees that appear from a distance to be a sail. The next town, Krou Settra, was known by a stand of high, bare trees that rose above it like the masts of laid up vessels, and the *Man and Wife Rocks* two miles from shore.[29] There was ivory to be found there and they lingered for some time while the captain located and purchased all that he could.

Eventually, they sailed for Young Sesters some 50 miles further along the Krou Coast to the southeast known by a large, black rock called *The Carpenter* one mile off the point.[30] They arrived here in January of 1789, by chance meeting up with the *Royal Charlotte*, John Guttridge, Master, out of Bristol. Having learned by this time that William Huddy was unable to safely navigate the treacherous reefs and shoals of the West African coast, and was unqualified to serve in the position for which he'd been hired, Connor made it known that he was in want of a first mate.

The *Royal Charlotte* had left Bristol one year earlier, on January 7, 1788, and was bound for home.[31] Connor was surely delighted to learn that Captain Guttridge's Second Mate, Josiah Jackson, was an American who held no particular interest in returning to England. Jackson agreed to be transferred to the *Mary*, increasing the number on board to six, including Connor; still one man short of a proper crew. But Guttridge had needs of his own and held that he could not spare Jackson unless he was replaced by another. Jacob Blackman, stricken earlier at Pocum by the same fever that killed Alex, had been away from home serving under a brutal master for 16 months. Recognizing a golden opportunity when he saw one, Blackman readily agreed to return to Bristol with the *Royal Charlotte*.

Josiah Jackson's first port of call as the *Mary's* new first mate was Krou Settra, where Connor hoped to add to his ivory hoard. Finding none, the captain's dark side returned. He became abusive toward the crew, reduced their rice ration to one pint each per day, and ordered Jackson to set sail for Anamabo, 550 miles to the east. It would be a suitable test to challenge the credentials of his new first mate.

En route to Anamabo they laid up briefly at Cape Lahou while Connor traded for ivory but quickly got underway again, passing Cape Three Points from a distance of nine or ten miles offshore owing to extremely rapid currents that break on a nearby reef. The site consists of three promontories with a distance of over three miles between their extremities and, except for two sandy bays, the shore is rocky. A Dutch fort stood on the easternmost projection of land.[32]

About 50 miles E.N.E. beyond Cape Three Points, the whitewashed walls of Cape Coast Castle, rising from a rock prominence of but 20 feet above sea level, were constantly buffeted by a heavy surf. This was the principal British fort on the Gold Coast and residence of England's chief governor during the sovereignty of the African Company. It spanned 180 yards[33], stood three stories high, mounted 80 cannon, garrisoned 200 soldiers, and cast its shadow on Cape Coast Town, which was known for the quality and quantity of its gold dust and was a major slave port.[34]

Yet another British fort was located on the coast 12 miles further to the northeast at Anamabo, between two more Dutch forts, one several miles to the west at Mauree, and the other about the same distance to the east at Cormantine. There is good anchorage in these waters and both the British and Dutch carried on a brisk trade here in slaves and gold.[35]

Finally arriving at Anamabo, Captain Connor went ashore. That night William Huddy, humiliated and angry for having been replaced by Jackson, took his chest and jumped ship. Following Connor's return, several natives came aboard and said they knew where Huddy was and would bring him back for a reward, which they did the next morning. But while aboard one of the natives slipped below unseen and stole cloth from the hold.

Later that day, Connor became aware of the theft and blamed Bird, accusing him of failing to keep watch while the natives were returning Huddy and collecting their reward. Connor knocked Bird to the deck with the pump brake handle, and then turned to Huddy promising to take the natives' reward from his wages. He then ordered Jackson to take the *Mary* back to Cape Lahou, some 200 miles to the west.

Approaching Cape Lahou, Connor ordered Bird to bring the *Mary* about beside a Dutch ship anchored offshore, but the currents were strong and they fell to leeward. Connor turned on Bird once again, beating him with ropes and the pump brake handle, promising Bird he would kill him if he failed to bring the *Mary* about as ordered by the next night. But the best that Bird could manage was to bring her to within a musket shot of the Dutch ship. Connor asked Bird if he had an anchor ready, and Bird said he did not because he could not free the anchor rope from under a puncheon of rum. Bird called to the other hands for help, but Connor demanded that he do it himself. He tried, but failed, and Connor then beat him again.

The other hands finally managed to free the anchor and at about four that afternoon a boat from the Dutch ship came for Connor and took him to meet with their master. It was between eight and nine in the evening when Connor returned, and he had been drinking.[36] As he climbed aboard, he invited Jackson to dine with him, and then went below to his cabin.

That night, Captain John Connor was murdered and the *Mary* weighed anchor. Connor's body was thrown overboard most probably in an area known as the Bottomless Pit, which is more than 200 fathoms deep and lies about 30 miles east of Cape Lahou and three miles out to sea from the coast at Picaniny Bassam.[37] It was January 23rd, 1789, and of the *Mary's* crew that left England 16 months earlier, only Thomas Bird and Hans Hanson remained aboard.

§

III

The Middle Passage and Capture

In defiant repudiation of the late Captain Connor's decision to replace him as First Mate, William Huddy took command of the *Mary* and announced that his plan was to run her toward the South Seas and into the Portugeuse settlements at Brazil. First, however, they would need to replenish their fresh water and provisions. They tacked in a northeasterly direction for about 200 miles, to the east side of Cape Three Points, and anchored offshore from the village of Akataykie. There were two forts nearby, one

23

British and the other Dutch, but both very small[38] and as they had not yet called on this port, no one would be looking for Captain Connor. There they traded for pineapples and yams, filled their water casks, and stood to sea.

On the third day, Huddy confessed that he was lost and asked Jackson for direction but Jackson, employing cunning to his best advantage, refused. Huddy went to the captain's cabin and returned with charts and a brace of pistols, one in his hand and the other at his side, and told Jackson to take command and carry them to America or, Huddy promised, the first time Jackson slept he would Jones[*] him. Once again, Jackson declined, but relented when Huddy offered to allow him to take the *Mary* to whatever port he chose, and give him a bill of sale for the vessel and its cargo, which he did.

Jackson immediately turned the *Mary* back toward the Guinea Coast and brought her to anchor off Ningo, a trade port about 100 miles east of Anamabo that rests on the shore seven miles west of the River Volta. The entire coast in this area is low, thickly wooded, and marshy. Far inland are the Crobo Mountains of which the sugarloaf-shaped Ningo Grande is the tallest and is easily distinguishable from the sea. Here the Danes had a sizable fort, and another on an island at the mouth of the Volta.[39]

---

[*] Consign him to Davy Jones' locker.

Ningo was yet another port where the *Mary* had not yet anchored on this voyage, and there would be no inquiries as to the whereabouts of Captain Connor. Jackson, however, may have been familiar with it and its traders. He and Bird went ashore there with trading goods and exchanged some cloth and gunpowder for ivory and a young Negro boy called Cuffey. When they returned they weighed anchor and on or about March 9th, 1789, the *Mary* tacked westward, toward the open sea. Jackson was a competent navigator and likely brought the vessel into the Equatorial Current as soon as possible until gaining some considerable distance to the west where he could pick up a northward current.[40]

On May 1st, 1789, somewhere in the Atlantic, William Huddy fell, or was pushed, overboard. Hanson, Huddy, and Cuffey stood watch that night. Both Bird and Jackson said they were asleep below. The next morning, Jackson woke Bird and asked him if he knew where Huddy was. Bird said he did not, but got up and helped Jackson search for him. They had all been drinking the night before and Hanson said Huddy was drunk. It was decided that Huddy had fallen into the sea.

In the following weeks, as they approached America's northeastern shore, they met up with two whaling vessels out of Bedford, Massachusetts, Francis Butler and John Mayhew, Masters. Jackson and Bird went aboard both, and dined on one of them, but Hanson and Cuffey remained on the *Mary* with four of the whaling crew to keep her close by. Later they met with an English ship and tender bound for the West Indies, and another outbound from Philadelphia. After taking soundings on the east end of Georges Bank they met with another vessel from Boston bound for Liverpool. Though they spoke with each of them, they boarded none of these.

The first land they made was Matinicus Island, 20 miles east of what was then Shore Village[*] at Lermond's Cove near Thomaston, Maine. On Friday, July 17th, 1789, they dropped anchor off of an elliptical strand of beach known as Cape Cove in the town of Cape Elizabeth, Maine.[†] Their passage from Ningo on Africa's Guinea Coast had taken four months and eight days.

For three days following their arrival at Cape Cove they traded guns, powder, knives, brass and pewter pans and kettles, bolts and pieces of India calico and patterned cloth, handkerchiefs, waist jackets, and sundry other items with the local people in exchange for food, spirits, and other comforts.[41] They sat about a campfire with the men who lived nearby telling stories of the African slave trade and of the exotic secrets hidden at the farthest ends of Africa's wild rivers and within its lush, dark jungles. The local people wondered who they really were and why they were anchored at Cape Cove, but agreed they seemed a friendly lot, with fine stories and even finer trade goods, which they offered at a fair exchange.

---

[*] Now the city of Rockland, Maine.
[†] Now Willard Beach in the city of South Portland, Maine.

There was at least one among the local people, however, whose suspicions weighed heavily on his mind. On Monday, July 20th, someone reported the *Mary's* presence to Nathaniel Fadre Fosdick, the local naval officer and collector of customs.[42] Revenue laws prohibited the undocumented trade that both the crew and the locals were engaged in, and Fosdick immediately rode to Cape Elizabeth with the intention of seizing the foreign sloop and her crew. To his surprise, none of the local inhabitants would assist him in boarding the vessel; on the contrary, they helped Jackson and his crew get the *Mary* underway and then piloted her out to sea.[43]

Fosdick returned to Portland, assembled two volunteer crews, and commandeered a sloop and a schooner to pursue the fugitives. They sailed that evening, and the next afternoon the schooner, commanded by Captain John Baker, came upon the *Mary*, which was anchored at Cape Porpoise, just 25 miles south of Portland Harbor. Jackson and his crew members did not anticipate Fosdick's fervor and, taken completely by surprise, they struck without resistance. Fosdick took the prize to Portland Harbor and on Wednesday, July 22nd, impounded the vessel with the court, and turned Jackson, Bird, Hanson, and Cuffey over to Colonel John Waite, Sheriff of Cumberland County, who detained them pending further instructions from the court.

THE MIDDLE PASSAGE AND CAPTURE

On Thursday, July 23rd, the Supreme Judicial Court of the Commonwealth of Massachusetts,* then seated in Portland, charged Jackson, Hanson, and Bird with ". . . feloniously and Pyratically stealing, and runing [sic] away upon the high Seas, with a small Sloop of about Thirty Tons, now lying and being at Portland . . . being the Property of some Person or Persons, who are as yet unknown."[44] The same day, Jackson and Hanson were examined before the court. The questions that each of the three men were asked during their examinations were not recorded. Hans Hanson's responses were recorded as set below:[†]

> Mr. Bradbury began to take the Minutes of the Examination & proceeded so far as to take down the Names of the Hands which sailed in said sloop from Plymouth in England which were as follows:
>
> Capt. Connor
> Morgan – mate
> Alex. – {I add from the Examined that he died on shore
> Thomas Bird
> Ned – ran away

PORTLAND NECK

Capt.
Jacob – {exchanged for Jackson the now

Jack – Discharged

Hans Hanson – the Examined

(So far Mr. Bradbury.)

The Examined said they went to the Island of Saloes on the coast of Guinea to look for Elephants Teeth. When they arrived at Saloes they spoke [to] the Factory Ship, who advised them to go up the River and purchase Slaves; they proceeded accordingly and took some Slaves on board which they afterwards sold to some Danes. They were at an Harbor called Cape Lahoo, when they found a Dutch Ship. This was in Novr or Decr last. Their Capt. Went on board the Dutch Ship there and afterwards returned when he told them there was war in the Country & that they must run up and lay along side of the Dutch Factory Ship, where they might be protected. They took Jackson the present Capt on board at an Harbor on the Coast of Guinea as a Mate, for whom they changed Jacob. They began to talk of destroying the Capt. When he was on a Pint, on board the Dutch Factory Ship, at Cape Lahoo. Jackson, the present Capt., got up brandy: Thomas Bird got up two guns, and said to Huddy there are two guns for you and two guns for me and they fired down the Cabin and down the Scuttle, over the Tiller, and killed the Capt.

29

They then got a light, and called up Jackson, and they then went down into the Cabin and took the Capt. And threw him overboard, Bedcloths and all. Thomas fired first and Huddy afterwards, almost at the same time. The Guns were loaded with Powder and Musket Balls. The next morning they went to a place call Yakee-Yakes [Akataykie]. Jackson took the command after the Capt. Was killed. After they had gotten Pineapples and yams on board, they stood to Sea for Boston. They afterwards went to a Danish Factory on the Coast called Ningo, and exchanged some cloth and Powder for Ivory and a little negro Boy called Cuffey. They had a Passage of 4 months & 8 Days to Cape Elizabeth. Will. Huddy fell overboard drunk. Cape Elizabeth was the first Port they made. They have not been on board any Vessel but two whalemen; but they spake two other Vessels as they passed the Gulph. Almost two months before they left the coast the Capt. Was killed. He [Hans Hanson] was born in Norway. The Capt's Name was John Connor, he lived in Virginia Street No. 77 London. The Capt. And one Clark and Hadley owned the Vessel, which was laden with paint, cloth, Powder, small arms, Butter, & some cheeses, & Brass Pans & Kettles. They bespoke two whalemen to whom they said they were bound for Boston the names of the Captains of the whalemen were Capt. Butler & Capt. Mayhew whose Vessels were a Brig and a Schooner. He thinks the Log

Book is on board. Jackson kept the Log book. He [Hans] is 19 years old. Several pieces of striped cloth has [sic] been bro't on shore from their Sloop, and sold to make Shirts. They bought their Ivory of the Danish Governor at Ningo for cloth.

Prisoner was then remanded.[45]

Josiah Jackson's responses were recorded as set below:

I sailed Jan. 7, 1788, in the Royal Charlotte from Bristol to the Coast of Africa, John Guttridge, Master, and I Mate. I remained on board on ye Cost [sic] of Africa till Jan. 7, 1789, when we met with ye Sloop John Connor, Master. Guttridge being bound home, & Connor being in want of a Mate. I entered on board ye sloop accordingly. The Ship then left ye Coast & we ran down to Cape Lahoo for Ivory. Then our Capt. Went on board a Dutch Ship & he returned abot [sic] 8 at night & turned in. Abot 12 at night or before day, Bird informed me he had killed ye Captain & Huddy told me the same & had joined in it. I wouldn't believe 'em & asked Huddy if he was dead, he said yes & overboard. I told Huddy he had taken ye vessel & he must carry her to some port. We were at this time at Anab° [Anamabo] on the Coast. Connor I found by papers on board was of London in Virginia Street. Huddy refused to take the command. I did the same. Huddy said he he w^d [would] run her into the S°. Seas to the Portuguese settlements. We accordingly ran to 6" S° Lat: 10 or 11 E. Long: Then he delivered the vessel to me & told me I might carry her to any port, & he w^d give a bill of sale of vessel & cargo to me and did so. Huddy kept the Log book till this time: after this I kept it till our arrival on this Coast. My intention was to go into Boston & make compl^t [complaint] of 'em.

Huddy was lost the 1st May in ye night. I know not how. It was his watch & Hans Hanson & ye Negro boy's. I was turned in. We met two American whaling vessels Francis Butler & John Mayhew of Bedford, Masters. I went on board of 'em twice. Afterwards We met with an Engh [sic] & [tender?] vessel but did not go on board either. It was calm but spoke 'em. The Engh vessel was bound to the West Indies.

We spoke to other ships from Philadelphia outward bound the Master's name I don't know. We didn't go on board. After soundings on ye East end of Georges, spoke another ship from Boston for Liverpool, out three days last Tuesday fortnight. The first Land we made was Matinikus [sic]. I left the Log Book in ye Cabbin when the vessel was taken at Cape Porpoise. I was at Saco. It is my writing from ye time I took ye command.

We arrived at Cape Eliz^a last fryday [sic] afternoon & remained till Monday P.M. Then*

32

we went for Cape Porpoise where we arrived abot 3 P.M. I went on shore same afternoon lodged at my brother's. The next morn^g I went to Saco & carried all our papers viz. a bill of Sale of the vessel from the Carpenter who built her in England to Capt. Connor. The bill of Sale of the vessel & cargo from Huddy to me. I showed the officer these at the Register & bills of laden. I went to make my entry as Master by the name of Josiah Jackson which is my name. I was born at Newton near Cambridge my father's name is Joshua Jackson. When I first entered the Sloop there were Bird, Huddy, Hans, and a young lad that went on board the ship in my stead. The Negro now on board I bot [sic] at Ningo Grandy [sic] on the Coast of Guinea. I didn't go on shore there. It was a Danish settlement. There are only two white Men there. Bird s^d [said] he stood at the Scuttle on ye quart^r deck & shot ye Capt: being asleep on his Cot frame in the Cabbin. Huddy s^d he fired two guns at him from the Hatchway at the same time. I was lay^g asleep on deck by the windlass. The crew were all sober when I went to sleep. I didn't hear any firing. I examined the Cabbin cou'd [sic] find no marks of balls, but I saw blood on ye floor & locker. This was the next morn^g abot sunrise. I didn't give any information to any of the vessels we spoke with of our situation or to any one after I came on shore at Cape Elizabeth or Cape Porpoise. My design was to go into Boston & do it there.

[*] being told we were in danger of being jailed by
ye Naval Officer for having lain there too long
with[t] [without] entering.[46]

Josiah Jackson was not remanded though extant court
records do not indicate that the charges against him were
dropped. His brother, Joshua, owned land in the town of
Arundel,[47] near Cape Porpoise, and might have secured
Josiah's release in exchange for collateral placed on his
property. Under the provisions of the Massachusetts Body
of Liberties of 1641, bail was guaranteed to all accused
persons except those charged with a capital crime or
contempt in open court,[48] though there is no record of bail
being set for Jackson either. It seems most likely that
Jackson struck a deal with the court.

According to Samuel Freeman, a native of Portland and a
clerk of the courts in Cumberland County during the time
of the trial, Jackson "was improved as a witness, whose
testimony, with the voluntary confession of *Bird,* taken in
writing, before the Supreme Judicial Court . . . and some
other circumstances . . . appeared satisfactory to the jury
to return a verdict . . ." (italics in the original).[49] While it
is true that Bird's "confession" was taken in writing, Bird
did not sign it or put his mark on it. On the last of three
handwritten pages there is a notation in the left margin
that reads "Bird's Exam" followed by "S. J. Court",

signifying Supreme Judicial Court. The initials "W.G." also appear here.

No further reference to the African boy, Cuffey, has been revealed. Whether he was kept at the jail during the period of Jackson's incarceration, or was taken to the Arundel home of Joshua Jackson, Josiah's brother, is not known. It seems likely, however, that when Josiah Jackson was released, the court would have placed Cuffey in his custody as he claimed to be his owner.

On July 24th, the day after Hanson and Jackson were examined, Thomas Bird was brought before the court. His responses were recorded as set below:

> I shipd [sic] in the Mary at Plym°: Jn°: Connor Master we had seven hands viz. the Capt: Tho Morgan Ch Mate, Edw°: Tool, Hans Hanson & Alex°: & John. I don't know their surnames & myself. We sailed Sept 1787 for the Coast of Africa and made land in 9 Weeks. We then put part of our Goods in the Tyger, an Engh Factory ship in Bodee's of London employ. Tho. Bullen was the Com: [Commander] on shore & on board as the Factor.
>
> We then went up ye River   to Tho. Orman's Store abot 50 Miles. There we landed some Copper we carried out for him. Then we went up Napongus River abot 12 Miles from the other. There we traded for Ivory & Slaves we took. Then we went to the Island Salos & sold

& delivered 'em to the Tyger Factor. We were abot 18 Mo: on ye Guinea Coast. Our Capt. Went on shore there better than a Mo: & found all hands asleep at 11° at night. He took up ye pump brake & struck Morgan with it & asked why he didn't keep watch, & jumped on his breast. afterw ye Capt: turned in. Morgan died ye next day. The Capt ordered Edw Tool to sew him in his Cot & throw him overboard. We all refused till the people might come & see him, from ye ship. He sd if we wdnt he wd give all of us ye same & began to beat Ted with ye pump break [*sic*]. He jumped over & swam ashore & never returned. We then, threw [sic] fear of ye Capt, obeyed & threw Morgan overboard abot 4° ye P.M. That P.M. the Capt went ashore & brot James & Sam, American Molattoes [*sic*]. We sailed ye next day to Lahoo abot 70 leagues. We remained there abot a fortn^t: & bot a pancheon [*sic*] of Rum. We then sailed for ye Ivory Coast at a place called Bumford where Alex died of Sickness on shore. We then went to Cape Mount where Molattoes ran away at night ye Capt got them before the next day. He then beat & abused everyone. We went from thence to Young Sesters where ye Capt sold 'em to Dutch ships for goods.

We then went to Grand Sesters & bot Ivory. We then returned to young Sesters. Here we met a Bristol Ship, Capt Guttridge, the Royal Charlotte. Here we took Jackson on board &

sent Jacob Blackman in his place. After
Morgan's death we took in Wm. Huddy as Mate
at the time we had the Molattoes. We went to
Crews Cettra [Krou Settra], there we bot Ivory.
The Capt then beat us & half starved us being
cross because he cdnt buy Ivory. He reduced us
to a pint of Rice per day.

Then we went to Cettra Crews [Settra Krou] &
got some Ivory. Then we returned back. There
Huddy went ashore in ye night & carried away
his chest & things. The Negroes came on board
& sd they wd bring him back. They did the next
morn^g. They stole cloth & the Capt abused me
for not prevent^g 'em. He knocked me down
with ye pump brake. He told Huddy he shd take
out of his wages what he had pd ye Negroes for
bringing him. At Cape Lahoo we fell to
Leeward. The Capt sd twas my fault & he wd
take my life if he we didn't catch up ye next
night. He beat me then fully for not doing it
with the pump brake & ropes . We got up
abot a Muske^t shot of a Dutch ship. The Capt:
then beat me again because we didn't get
nearer. A boat came from the Dutch ship &
carried him on board abot 4° P.M. he stayed till
dark then the Mate Jackson & Capt went to
supper in the Cabbin. After Jackson came & laid
down on deck by the Windlass & went to sleep.
The Capt: came up soon after abot 9° even^g: &
asked if I had a anchor ready to let go. I told
him no. I coud [sic] not get the rope free

from under a pancheon. I was going to ask for hands to help me & he told me to do it myself. I sd I coudnt myself but went down & tried but coudn't. I sta'd in the Hatchway & the Capt. Went into the Cabbin to sleep. Hanson, Huddy & myself killed him   night. The Capt: was killed by Musket balls fired out of one gun which the Capt: had loaded that afternoon. There were three guns in all fired at him. I then abot 12 or 1 at night assisted in throwing him over. Wm. Huddy, Hanson & myself did it. Jackson was asleep & had been so from the time he went forward as above. Huddy took the command, in abot three days after, Huddy s^d he wd go to ye Brazil, we run towards ye Brazil till he said he didn't know where he was. He brot up ye papers & a brace of Pistols one in his hand ye other at his side & told Jackson he must take the command & carry her to America or the first time he slept he woud Jones him as he had done the Capt. Jackson declined it telling him he had ye command & might carry her where he woud.   He then insisted upon Jackson's taking the command & delivered him the papers only but kept the pistols. At last Jackson consented & altered our course for America. We made Ningo Grandy on the African Coast unexpectedly. There Huddy & I went on shore with goods & bot the Negro Boy now with us. After when we were sailing for America on the 2^d May in ye morning I missed Wm. Huddy. Jackson missed Huddy first & came & waked me

& asked if I knew where Huddy was. I told him no. I got up & search'd for him with Jackson but coudnt find any thing of him. We thought he was fallen over for we had all been drink[g]. It was Huddy & Hanson's watch ye night before. The next day I was breaking a Cocoa Nut with ye Ax & Hanson said   sounded liked Huddy's head when he struck him the first time with it and that he had killed him with ye ax. I asked what he did it for he s[d] because he now sh'd live a happy life for Jackson he knew w'd not beat him. I have seen Huddy tie up Hanson several times & beat him very much with ropes. We after went on board two American Whalemen. Jackson went first & I after. We dined on board of them at this time. Hanson & the Negro boy remain[d] in our sloop and four of the whaling crew to keep her close to them. We   two of their boats. Jackson told them he was bound from Africa for Boston. That we had lost one hand Huddy overboard but said nothing abot Capt. Connor's death. We had told him he had been killed the morn[g] after it happened.[50]

The Supreme Judicial Court instructed Sheriff Waite to take an inventory of every item on the *Mary*, and if it appeared that the men in custody had disposed of property to any inhabitants of the county, Waite was to recover the items or report the names of such persons to the court. Four days later, on July 27th, Waite submitted the inventory to the court, which included 197 yards of cloth of various colors and descriptions; 96 small kegs, 16 large kegs, and 1 barrel of powder; a 3 gallon cask of palm oil; 2 casks of butter; 3 kegs of paint; 99 brass rods; 254 brass pans and kettles; 30 pewter basins; 78 flat bars of iron; 34 dozen knives; several barrels of beef and pork; a container of grains of paradise;* 9 pairs of iron shackles; 1 firelock; 1 pistol; 169 elephants' tusks; and assorted and sundry other goods and wares. The inventory also listed tackle, tools, and other equipment commonly found on merchant vessels, and estimated the total value of the items inventoried to be 456 pounds, 4 shillings.

On the fifth and final page of the inventory it is noted that "(t)he price of the Elephants Teeth & of the Grains of Paradise we were totally Ignorant of, but governed our Judgment in some measure by a London price current for the year 1785." The document was signed by John Waite, Sheriff, and witnessed by Enoch Ilsley, William Vaughn, and Samuel Pierson.[51]

Nearly three weeks later, on August 15th, Sheriff Waite submitted to the court an itemized list of unrecovered goods and wares received by 38 residents of Cape Elizabeth, and 2 residents of Scarborough, including 12 members of the Jordan family, 6 McKennys, and 4 Robinsons, all of Cape Elizabeth. These items included 6

---

* An exotic African pepper.

guns, 10 kegs of powder, and 12 knives, as well as brass kettles, paint, pieces of cloth, and other sundries.[52]

A maritime or admiralty judge assigned to each of the Supreme Judicial Courts of the several states in the Union was authorized to try cases defined as piracy or felony on the high seas. The Massachusetts Legislature had enacted the law in February of 1783. It was in anticipation of such a trial that Thomas Bird and Hans Hanson were remanded to the custody of Sheriff Waite and they were confined in the Cumberland County Jail.

Forty-three years earlier, in 1746, a blockhouse was built in Haymarket Square* to protect the inhabitants of Portland Neck against Indian attacks. When a peace treaty ending the French and Indian wars was signed in 1763, the garrison was of no further use and it was sold to the county for use as a jail. A jail-keeper's house was later "built on Middle Street, in front of the jail, in which the jailer kept a public house, as the county paid him only fifteen pounds as jailer."[53]

Before the next session of the Supreme Judicial Court was held in Cumberland County, the U.S. Congress passed the Judiciary Act and, on September 24th, 1789, President George Washington signed it into law. The measure established federal district and circuit courts, and a U.S. Supreme Court. Piracy, felony, and all other capital offenses committed on the high seas were committed to

---

*   Now Monument Square.

the jurisdiction of the Federal Circuit Court, and all the powers of the Circuit Court were given to the Federal District Court of Maine, effectively transferring authority in the case concerning Bird and Hanson from the Supreme Judicial Court of Massachusetts, to the Federal District Court of Maine. The officers of the new Federal District Court of Maine, however, had not yet been appointed. [54]

On September 26th, two days after President Washington signed the Judiciary Act into law, he commissioned Judge David Sewall, 53, of York, Maine, as judge of the U.S. Court for the District of Maine. [55] Sewall had served as a judge of the Supreme Judicial Court of Massachusetts since 1781 and was undoubtedly one of the judges before whom Jackson, Bird, and Hanson had been examined. [56] During the Revolutionary War, David Sewall served as a captain of the 2nd Military Company of Foot. [57]

Judge Sewall took the oath of his new office on December 1, 1789, before Samuel Freeman, Richard Codman, John Frothingham, and Daniel Davis, Justices of the Peace. The same day he called his court into session for the first time and administered the oath of office to the other newly appointed U.S. District Court of Maine officers: U.S. Marshal Henry Dearborn, 38, of Monmouth; District Attorney William Lithgow, Jr., 38; and Clerk of the Court Henry Sewall, 36, both of Fort Western. [58]

Marshal Henry Dearborn was a physician, had served as an officer throughout the Revolutionary War, and was discharged with the rank of colonel. In 1787, he was

42

commissioned a major general in the Maine Militia.[59] District Attorney William Lithgow, Jr. also served as an officer during the revolution. He was discharged in 1777 with the rank of major after receiving a serious wound to his elbow at Saratoga, which permanently disabled his right arm. In 1787, he too was commissioned a major general in the Maine Militia.[60] Clerk of the Court Henry Sewall, a cousin to Judge David Sewall, enlisted in the army as a private to fight in the revolution and served through the war rising to the rank of captain of infantry. In 1787, he was commissioned a colonel in the 8th Division of the Maine Militia serving under Maj. Gen. William Lithgow, Jr.[61]

During the second session of Judge Sewall's U.S. District Court, which was held in Pownalborough* in March of 1790, arrangements were made for a grand and three full petit juries to be summonsed for the court's third session.[62] If the grand jury handed up an indictment, Bird and Hanson would be tried on June 4, 1790, following confinement in the Cumberland County Jail for nearly a year.

---

* Now Wiscasset, Maine.

THE TRIAL

IV

The Trial

Thomas Motley had been the Cumberland County Jailer since 1781. To supplement his income, which was but £15 per year, he and his family lived in and operated a tavern built on Middle Street in front of the jail. An overhead, swinging sign at the front of the tavern bore the words "Freemason's Arms" and was inscribed with the square and compasses of Freemasonry.[63] Motley was married to Sheriff John Waite's younger sister, Emma, and they had seven children, all boys, the youngest born in 1785.[64]

Little is known of Thomas Bird, and less of Hans Hanson, during the months of their confinement in Portland. But it has been noted that Thomas and Emma Motley came to hold Bird in rather high regard. They allowed their sons to visit Bird in his jail cell, though the youngest, Charles, was but five years of age. Bird passed much of his time carving toy ships and boats for the boys. The Motleys' trust and affection for Bird was such that they had no fear of harm to their children, though Bird had a carving knife and could have attempted to escape. The old wooden jail was always in need of repairs and prisoners frequently escaped from it.[65]

The new Cumberland County Court House, finished in 1788, was a two-story wooden building measuring 48 feet by 34 feet located on Back Street about 400 yards east of the jail.[*] At the front of the building a whipping-post stood as a clear and constant reminder of the painful price paid for disregard of the law. The first floor was an open hall where a gallows and stocks were kept in plain view. A court room and offices were on the second floor, and a belfry was added, above which a carved weathercock was mounted. "St. Peter's testimony in denying his Master may have suggested to the county fathers the propriety of surmounting the new temple of justice with a representative of the historic bird, as a caution to the witness, when he entered the portal, not to deny the truth, whatever might be the provocation from contending counsel."[66]

On or about June 1, 1790, District Attorney Lithgow and Marshal Dearborn arrived at Portland. They had ridden together from Fort Western, a settlement on the Kennebec River, some 60 miles to the northeast.[67] Nearly a full year had passed since the capture of the *Mary* and

---

[*] Now the site of Portland City Hall on Congress Street.

her crew, and on June 1, a Tuesday, Lithgow presented the case to a federal grand jury. Benjamin Titcomb, a deacon of the First Parish Church and a local blacksmith, was appointed to serve as its foreman. The grand jury found one bill against Thomas Bird, charging that he "piratically, feloniously, willfully and of his malice afore-thought did kill and murder" Captain John Connor on the high seas, and another bill against Hans Hanson, charging that he "knowingly and willingly did aid, abet and assist" Thomas Bird in that crime.[68]

The next day, Marshal Dearborn escorted Bird and Hanson to their arraignment at the court house where the indictment was read to them. Both of the prisoners pleaded not guilty and "put themselves upon the country".[69] The court assigned John Frothingham and William Symmes, both local attorneys, to defend the accused, and provided them with a copy of the indictment, and a list of the panel of jurors who would hear the case.

On Friday morning, June 4th, Judge Sewall arrayed in a white, powdered wig and black silk robe,[70] convened the third session of the U.S. District Court of Maine, but immediately recessed so the venue could be moved to the First Parish Meeting House located approximately midway between the court house and the jail. The new court house was far too small to accommodate the curious crowd that had gathered to witness the trial and was anxiously milling about in the street demanding entry.[71]

The court was soon reconvened at the Meeting House and a jury of 12 men was seated: Deacon Amos Chase of Little Ossipee Town[*], Foreman; Humphrey Chase, and Asa Lewis, both of North Yarmouth; Samuel Whitmore of Gorham; George Knight III, Joshua Stevens, Robert Clemmons, and Nathaniel Wilson, all of Falmouth; Josiah Fairfield of Pepperellborough[†]; Micah Dyar, and Daniel Strout, town or towns unknown.[‡] [72]

The defendants' examinations were read and to the extent that it was possible and legally proper John Frothingham and William Symmes addressed the court using words carefully chosen in an attempt to create plausible doubt. William Lithgow, Jr. was next to speak assuring the court the evidence would establish a certainty of guilt. Then Josiah Jackson "was improved as a witness"[73] and testified before the court. Unfortunately, his words were not recorded and his testimony is lost to history. The trial lasted five hours[74] and following closing arguments the jury considered the evidence presented as it appeared in the light and shadows cast by their individual lives and experiences.

"(A)bout the close of the same day,"[75] the jury returned with its verdicts. They found Thomas Bird guilty as charged and Hans Hanson not guilty. Hanson was

---

[*] Now Limington.

[†] Now Saco.

[‡] U.S. Census for the State of Maine, 1790, was used to establish the residency of 10 jurors.

immediately released and Judge Sewall, attempting to speak above the roar of the clamoring crowd, announced that Bird was being placed in the custody of Marshal Dearborn to be returned to the jail house until the following morning. The court would then reconvene at the court house and Bird's sentence would be pronounced.

Saturday morning, June 5th, the first item of business considered by the court was a motion in arrest of judgment made by William Symmes, who argued "first, The Bill against the said Bird, is not found by the Jurors of the United States; secondly, The place where the crime is said to be comitted (sic), is uncertain; thirdly, The Indictment does not conclude, against the peace and dignity of the United States, as it ought to do". Judge Sewall considered the motion and ruled it "insufficient to arrest the Judgment."[76]

Judge Sewall continued:

> You Thomas Bird, unhappy prisoner at the bar, have been charged by a Grand Jury of this District of piratically murdering, on the high seas, *John Conner*. To this charge you plead *not guilty*, and put yourself on trial. And a Jury duly appointed, impannelled [*sic*] and sworn, after a candid public hearing (in which every indulgence, directed or permitted by the humane laws of the land, has been improved in your behalf to manifest your innocence) have declared you GUILTY. – The Attorney for this district has, in the name and behalf of the

49

United States, moved this Court that Sentence of Death, for the crime of which you stand convicted, may be passed upon you. And nothing has been offered by your Council sufficient to arrest the sentence. – This painful and disagreeable task it now becomes the duty of this Court to discharge. The evidence that has appeared upon this trial, must fully satisfy every one that heard it, of the justness of the verdict against you; and your own conscience must fully assent to its impartiality.

You have, with a degree of deliberation generally unusual in the commission of such an atrocious offence, embrued [*sic*] your hands in the blood of one of your fellow men. A man under whom, by your voluntary agreement, you were placed; and who, by the regulations of society, it was your duty to have protected from injury and violence. This man you have murdered in bed, while endeavouring to recruit and refresh himself in the way and manner which nature dictates and directs.

Although the deed was done under the darkness of the night, yet it is now made public and manifest in the face of day. You hastened him from time to eternity, without any notice or even time to put up a single petition to the great Creator and Preserver of men. You in this respect have not the same measure meted to you, that you meted to the unfortunate *Conner:* – For in addition to the time already had, since your apprehension and commitment, you will have a few days more to ask mercy and forgiveness of that God whose laws, as well as the laws of society, you have so flagrantly violated. – "Whosoever sheddeth man's blood, by man shall his blood be shed," is a precept of the Divine Being very anciently promulgated – a precept pretty universally adopted by nations, whether civilized or barbarous.

You are now to be cut off by the hand of public justice, as unfit and dangerous to society – as an example to deter others from the commission of such enormities; having justly forfeited your life by the laws of nature and nations. Remember that you are soon, very soon to appear before a Tribunal infinitely superiour to any on earth, where the crime you have now been convicted of, and all others by you committed during your whole life, however secret and hidden they may have been from the view of your fellow men, will be made naked and evident – that unless by sincere and unfeigned repentance, you obtain a pardon of your aggravated transgressions, unutterable woe and misery must be your final doom, in the place where hope never comes.

Let me therefore earnestly exhort you to cry continually to that Being whose holy and just laws you have broken, and into whose presence you are shortly to make your appearance, for mercy and forgiveness, through the merits of his only Son; and who has declared himself ready and willing to forgive the greatest of sinners, upon their sincere repentance. – And may you be so happy as to obtain his pardoning mercy and forgiveness; and escape a punishment, in kind and duration, infinitely beyond the power of human tribunals, to inflict.

The Sentence which the law has affixed to your crime, and which this Court now awards against you, is this, *That you go from hence to the prison from whence you came; and from thence to the place of Execution, on Friday, the twenty-fifth day of June instant; and there be hanged by the neck until you are dead.* [Italics in the original] – And may God Almighty have mercy on your soul.[77]

Thomas Bird was returned to the Cumberland County Jail, but his attorneys, John Frothingham and William Symmes, immediately set to work composing an application for pardon "on the ground of its being the first capital conviction in the United States Courts, after the adoption of the Federal constitution."

Portland in the District of Maine June the 5th 1790

Permit a stranger to inform your Excellency, that about twelve months since, I was apprehended & committed to Goal, in the Town of Portland, within the District of Maine, charged with the murder of Capt. John Conner, of the Sloop Mary, upon the Coast of Africa. That yesterday I was tried & found guilty of the Crime, & that the District Judge, a few hours since pronounced the fatal sentence, that still rings in my Ears & harrows up my soul, the sentence of Death, which is to be Executed upon me on the 25 day of June Inst., The time is short Great Washington, too short, for a wretch harden'd in Crimes to prepare for that Country, from whose bourn no Traveller e'er return'd. Permit him to intreat your Excellency, in your great Clemency, to grant him a Pardon or Commute the punishment to something, to any thing, short of Death, It is usual for Kings and Emperors, at the Commencement of their Reign to grant such indulgences, Permit me then to beg that the Commencement of your administration may be marked, by Extending mercy to the first Condemned under it, or at least by granting him a Reprieve for a few months longer, your Excellency will be pleas'd to consider that I am at a great distance from the seat of Government, and that the days I have to live are very few, so that my Case demands immediate attention, Hear then and immediately attend to the cries, of a wretch, who unless your Excellency interpose will before Saturday the 26. of this month be beyond the reach of your Excellency's goodness.[78]

The petition was immediately dispatched by rider to President Washington, who then lived in New York, but Washington declined pardoning Bird, or suspending the time of execution. [79]

President Washington later confirmed his decision in a letter to Judge Sewall:

> New York, June 28, 1790.
>
> Sir: I have to acknowledge the receipt of your letter of the 5th instant, enclosing a copy of the process of the district Court of Main [sic] against Thomas Bird for a capital offence.
>
> No palliating circumstance appeared in the case of this unhappy Man to recommend him to mercy for which, he applied: I could not therefore have justified it to the laws of my Country, had I, in this instance, exercised that pardoning power which the Constitution vests in the President of the United States. I am etc. [80]

V

The Execution

Between the hours of three and five on the afternoon of Friday, June 25, 1790, U.S. Marshal Henry Dearborn appeared at the Cumberland County Jail to deliver Thomas Bird to his fate. The jailer, Thomas Motley, and his family, had come to the opinion that Bird should have been pardoned, and it was with great sadness that he was surrendered to Marshal Dearborn. Mrs. Motley collected her seven sons and led them to the far northwest side of Portland Neck, beyond the sights and sounds of the gallows, where they may have passed some time playing in the waters of Back Cove with the wooden boats Bird had carved for them. Marshal Dearborn then relieved jailer

Thomas Motley of his charge and took Bird from the jailhouse and into Haymarket Square.

Mr. Isaac Gage, an accomplished vocalist who frequently performed at the First Parish services, and was much praised for his ability by Rev. Samuel Deane, led the procession singing hymns.[81] The crowd before them parted, and many solemnly accompanied Mr. Gage's requiem, as they marched to Haggett's Hill at the junction of Congress and Grove Streets where a gallows had stood since the town's first execution* in 1772.[82]

Though the population of Portland at this time was but 2,240 residents[83], it was estimated that 3,000 to 4,000 spectators gathered to witness the execution.[84] Thomas Bird's body was later laid to rest in an unmarked grave at what is now Portland's Eastern Cemetery. The location of the burial site is unknown.[85]

Thomas B. Wait, editor of Portland's *Cumberland Gazette*, had arranged to meet with Thomas Bird earlier on the day of execution and recorded the condemned man's final statement. Wait published the statement on a broadside, which he planned to offer for sale to the throng of spectators that he was certain would gather for the execution. A number of his newspaper subscribers argued, however, they had already paid for whatever news

---

* According to William Willis' *History of Portland*, a Mr. Goodwin was convicted of murdering a man by throwing him overboard from a boat in Casco Bay.

about town was worthy of printing, and they demanded that Bird's statement be published in the newspaper. Wait held out for four weeks, but on July 26 he conceded to their demands.

PORTLAND

The following account of the Life & Death of *Thomas Bird*, is published merely to oblige some few of our *kind* readers, who had rather quarrel with the Printer, than part with four Coppers — although the money should be appropriated to the gratification of their own curiosity.

_____

The **DYING SPEECH of THOMAS BIRD**, Executed at Portland, June 25, 1790, for the murder of Capt. John Connor, on board the Mary near the coast of Africa, taken from his mouth on the last day of his life.

I THOMAS BIRD, being 40 years old last November, was born of honest parents, George & Anne Bird, in the Parish of Aborslay [Abbotts Leigh], near Bristol, England. I suppose I have two brothers now living in the same Parish.

I was sent to school at about 8 years old, from which I immediately ran away, and went to sea

57

with my Uncle. After one voyage with him, I became an apprentice to one Capt. John Smith of Bristol, under whom I served seven years. After this, I followed the sea, as I happened to get employ, which was mostly to the West Indies, and the coast of Africa. In the first of last war, on board of Capt. James Smith, I was taken by a Marblehead Brig, and carried in there, whence I went to Boston, and was exchanged at Newyork [sic]. I went to Bristol and was soon pressed on board the Medea Frigate, where I served 10 months, ran away from her at Hull, and travelled to Liverpool. There I shipped aboard the brig Edward, Capt. Parks, bound to Newyork, taken by the brig General Glover and carried a second time into Marblehead. I sailed out of that place, and Salem, for three or four years. Toward the end of the war, I sailed in the Eagle Privateer, which was taken by the Hind of 20, and Wolfe of 40 guns, and carried to Quebeck [sic]. In three weeks I shipped aboard a brig bound to Scotland. In a month after my arrival there, I entered aboard the ship Ruby, bound to Newyork, Capt. Rankin. After my arrival there, I was pressed aboard an English ship called the Vulean, from which I soon deserted at Sandy Hook [New Jersey], travelled to Philadelphia, and shipped aboard a Brig, Capt. Thomas, bound to Teneriff, where the vessel was lost, on a reef of rocks. I then shipped aboard a Spanish Cutter, belonging to Cardiz, in which I continued ten months, and was discharged in Portugal. I shipped on board an English frigate at Lisbon bound to England, landed at Portsmouth, went to Liverpool, sailed thence to the coast of Africa, & returned to the same place. Afterwards I made another voyage to Africa in the ship Favourite, whence we carried slaves to the Westindies [sic] and returned to London. After one month I was pressed on board the Bombay lying at Portsmouth, in which I served 18 or 20 months, and was discharged.

In 6 or 7 day[s] I shipped aboard the Mary, Captain Connor, bound to the coast of Africa. We arrived after a long passage at the island of Salos, where we lay at anchor three or four days. Then we went to a place on a river called Lapongus, and staid about a week, where we delivered sheets of copper to Mr. Thomas Horman, who keeps a factory there. Edward [T]ool ran away from us at this place. We came back to Salos and staid about a week. From Salos we went up the river Keffey, bought rice there, and a few pieces of gold. Thence to Bumford river, and staid 3 or 4 weeks lying abreast a town called Pocum, where we purchased three slaves. Three of our men, Alex. Hans & Jack sickened & went ashore. Alex. Died, the other two got well, and came aboard at the town of Bumford. Morgan the mate died here. Capt. Connor came aboard when the mate was asleep, it being his watch; the Capt.

Struck him more than 20 stroakes [*sic*] with the pump-brake, of which blows he died next day. The Captain would not permit us to give him so much as water, tho' he cried much for it. Soon after we sailed again to the island of Salos, with 16 slaves on board; there we put our slaves on board a factory ship; took out all our cargo, stored it, hove down our vessel, and cleaned her bottom. Then took nine of the slaves, carried them to Salone, and sold them to a Danish ship, Capt. Cook, took goods for them, shipped one black and one white man, returned to Salos, where the Captain put the white man aboard and shipped another black man there, and Thomas Huddy as mate, and exchanged goods with a factory ship. Jack was taken sick and put ashore on a desolate island. We never heard of him again. Then we made sale for Cape Mount. We had now on board besides the Capt. Huddy, myself, Hans Hanson, Jacob Blackman, James and Sam two Molttoes [*sic*]. The Captain was sick a few days. In 3 weeks we arrived at the Cape. We got water bought ivory out of a Brig, and staid about a week. Here the molattoes and myself being abused by the Captain, ran away: we were stopped by the negroes, and brought aboard. The Capt. Put the two Molattoes in irons. The next day we sailed for Snow Bay, where we found a Dutch ship to whom we sold Sam and James; then made sale for Cruze Secra, purchased ivory there, and staid some time; and then went to the Grand

Sisters, and from thence to young Sisters. Here we saw Capt. Guttridge from Bristol, lying a little without us, with whom we exchanged Jacob for Josiah Jackson. Then went back to the Cruze, staid there one night, thence to Animaboo.

Here the Captain went aboard a Dutch ship, about 3 P.M. while he staid there, Jackson agreed to run away with the vessel that night, & leave the Captain. They made me swear on the prayer book, that I would never betray them; assuring me that when they got to Cape Porpus [sic] in New England, they would pay me my wages, and discharge me. The Captain came aboard before dark. Jackson supped with him. In the mean time I was laid down in the forecastle to sleep. After supper Jackson came and waked me, and asked whose watch it was. I said mine, if it was 8 o'clock. He said I need not get up till 4 o'clock, so I laid down and went to sleep. After sunrise, Jackson and Huddy waked me, calling on me to help heave up the anchor, which we did short, & set the mainsail. After the anchor was up, I asked them if they were not going to call up the Captain. I was answered, I think by both of them, he was up as much as he ever would be. I asked what was become of the Captain. Huddy answered, it was nothing to me. He was gone where he never would be seen or heard of again, or to that purpose.

THE EXECUTION

About two months after this, Huddy was missing, after the night of the first of May, 1789. I slept the whole of said night, and reason to think Hans did also. – I never was concerned in the murder of Capt. Connor, nor of any one else, nor knowing to his death. – I acknowledge I have lived an irreligious, wicked life, profaning the name of God, lying & drinking to excess. – I freely wish and pray for God's forgiveness to all men who have injured me, as I hope forgiveness of God through Jesus Christ my Lord.

As a dying Man I declare before God the above account to be strictly true. [Italics in the original.]

his

THOMAS † BIRD

mark

News of the capture of Josiah Jackson, Hans Hanson, and Thomas Bird was also reported in the following newspapers: (New York City) New York Daily Gazette,

August 1, 1789, page 742; (Portsmouth) New Hampshire Gazette, August 6, 2-3; (Providence, Rhode Island) United States Chronicle, August 6, 2; (Boston, Massachusetts) Herald of Freedom, August 7, 166; (New York, New York) Gazette of the United States, August 8, 135; (Hartford) Connecticut Courant, August 10, 3; (New Haven) Connecticut Journal, August 12, 2; (Philadelphia, Pennsylvania) Independent Gazetteer, August 13, 2; (Worcester) Massachusetts Spy, August 13, 3; (New York, New York) Daily Advertiser, August 13, 2; (New York, New York) Weekly Museum, August 15, 2; (Massachusetts) Boston Gazette, August 17, 4; (Windsor) Vermont Journal, August 19, 3; (Elizabethtown) New Jersey Journal, August 19, 3; (Keene) New Hampshire Recorder, August 20, 3; and (New London) Connecticut Gazette, August 21, 2.

The trial of Thomas Bird and Hans Hanson, and/or the execution of Thomas Bird was also reported in the following newspapers: (Worcester) Massachusetts Spy, June 10, 1790, page 3; (Boston, Massachusetts) Herald of Freedom, June 11, 103; (Portsmouth) New Hampshire Spy, June 12, 54; (Philadelphia, Pennsylvania) Federal Gazette, June 14, 2; (Philadelphia) Pennsylvania Packet, June 14, 2; (New York City) New York Packet, June 15, 2; (Massachusetts) Salem Gazette, June 15, 2; (Newburyport, Massachusetts) Essex Journal, June 16, 2; (Portsmouth) New Hampshire Gazette, June 17, 2; (New London) Connecticut Gazette, June 18, 2; (New York, New York) Daily Advertiser, June 19, 3; (Rhode Island) Providence Gazette, June 19, 3; (Philadelphia) Pennsylvania Packet,

June 21, 2; (Hartford, Connecticut) American Mercury, June 21, 3; (Hartford) Connecticut Courant, June 21, 3; (Stockbridge, Massachusetts) Western Star, June 22, 3; (Philadelphia, Pennsylvania) Freeman's Journal, June 23, 2; (Middletown, Connecticut) Middlesex Gazette, June 26, 1; (Windsor) Vermont Journal, June 30, 3; (New York, New York) Gazette of the United States, July 10, 518; and (Rhode Island) Providence Gazette, July 10, 3. [86]

Biographical Sketches of Key Figures in the Trial and Execution of Thomas Bird

Judge David Sewall

(1735 – 1825)

U.S. District Court Judge

for the District of Maine

David Sewall was born in York on October 7th, 1735, and graduated at Harvard College in 1755. For several years thereafter he studied law in Portsmouth, New Hampshire, with Judge William Parker, and in 1759 became an original proprietor of Wolfeborough, New Hampshire. Finding little work in a frontier settlement, he returned to York the following year and in 1762 married Mary Parker, daughter of his former mentor, who was five years his senior.

His law practice was very successful and in 1763 the Superior Court admitted him to the degree of Barrister. He was one of only six lawyers to be so privileged in the District of Maine.[1]

---

[1] William Willis, *A History of The Law, The Courts, and The Lawyers of Maine, from its First Colonization to the Early Part of the Present Century* (Portland, Maine: Bailey & Noyes, 1863), 123.

Appointed as captain of the York Militia's Second Military Company of Foot in 1772, David Sewall had an honorable but not particularly illustrious record of military service. There is no record of him having left the comfort of his hearth and home during the Revolutionary War, but apparently he was never very enthusiastic about the rebellion. In 1778 his good friend Jonathan Sayward confided to his diary that Judge Sewall was "more and more doubtful as to success [in] our controversy with the King." Nevertheless, he participated in the Constitutional Convention of 1779 and worked on several committees to revise the laws and to clear Maine land titles.

After the war he was appointed a judge of the Superior Court of Massachusetts, District of Maine, which in 1781 was renamed the Supreme Judicial Court. With the organization of the United States Government in 1789, he was commissioned judge of the U.S. District Court for the District of Maine. Vice President John Adams may well have been influential in Sewall's elevation as they had been classmates at Harvard. In his letter of acceptance he wrote the following to President Washington:

> In this new appointment, the Judge is to stand alone and unassisted in some instances in matters of the greatest magnitude – such as relate to the *life of man*. Some unhappy Persons [Thomas Bird and Hans Hanson] are now under confinement, within the District upon a charge of Pyracy [*sic*] and Felony on the

high Seas, and whose situation, will claim an early attention in this court.

But from the laws of the U.S. hitherto enacted, it strikes me some other provision is necessary to be made, before a trial of this nature, can with propriety be had; more especially in case of conviction, to have the Judgement [*sic*] carried into execution. These difficultys I shall take the liberty of stating to some Gen[tlemen], in the legislature, to the end they may be thus considered, rather than arrest your attention from the many other important business of the union.

Judge David Sewall was 54 years of age when he convened the trial of Thomas Bird and Hans Hanson. Two years earlier, on May 28, 1788, his wife, Mary, died of the "Numb Palsey"[2] brought on by a stroke. Though married more than 25 years, they were childless. Three months before the trial, his 94-year-old mother, Sarah Sewall, fell ill and died.[3] It was said that "(h)e was a learned and upright judge, – a man of great benevolence, unassuming in his deportment, sociable and amiable in his manners, and of great purity of character." It must have been with a heavy heart that he anticipated the possibility of presiding over a court that held the lives of two men in its balance.

---

[2] Paralysis.

[3] *"Salaries"*, Portland (Maine) Cumberland Gazette, 1 March 1790.

On November 21, 1790, five months after Thomas Bird's execution, Judge Sewall married his second wife, Elizabeth, the eldest daughter of Rev. Dr. Samuel Langdon of Hampton Falls, New Hampshire. This same year Judge Sewall was elected to the U.S. House of Representatives, but it was held by some that a federal judge could not be seated in the U.S. Congress and the opposition prevailed.

In 1794 he raised "his Grand new House" in York, which he called Coventry Hall. He and Elizabeth moved in three years later. Little children were brought here to have him "stroke away their warts, for he was the seventh son of a seventh son" and, according to Jonathan Sayward, he was "remarkably successful in this art."

David Sewall served as Judge of the U.S. District Court in Maine for more than 28 years, resigning January 9, 1818. In his resignation letter addressed to President James Monroe, he cited his "advanced years", he was then 83, and requested "relief from the cares of a publick nature." At this time he had been seated on the bench for more than 40 years.

He was a member of the Massachusetts Historical Society, but when Maine separated from Massachusetts in 1820 and he no longer qualified for membership, the society ignored the change in his status and his activity in helping to organize the Maine Historical Society. He died, childless, at York on October 22, 1825, at the age of 90. His widow, Elizabeth, died September 8, 1838. [4]

---

[4] Except as otherwise noted, all biographical information on Judge David Sewall taken from *Collections and Proceedings of the Maine Historical Society,* Second Series, Vol. II (Portland, Maine: Maine Historical Society, 1891), 301-17; and Clifford K. Shipton, *Sibley's Harvard Graduates Vol XIII 1751-1755: Biographical Sketches Of Those Who Attended Harvard College in the Classes 1751-1755 with Bibliographical and Other Notes* (Boston: Massachusetts Historical Society, 1965), 638-44.

William Lithgow, Jr.

(1750 – 1796)

U.S. District Attorney

for the District of Maine

William Lithgow, Jr., was born at Fort Halifax,[5] Maine, in 1750, one of Judge William and Sarah Lithgow's eleven children. Though he did not attend college, he was well educated and read law under James Sullivan, Esq., at Biddeford.

Lithgow was no stranger to Portland as he was garrisoned on The Neck in 1776 when a captain in command of a company of defenders within a few months after Captain Mowatt destroyed the town. In 1777, he was a major in the 11th Massachusetts Regiment when he received a serious wound at Saratoga. He was struck in the elbow by a musket ball, which permanently disabled his right arm.[6] For a period thereafter he served President George Washington as an aide-de-camp and was present at the surrender of British General John Burgoyne. Ten years later, Lithgow was commissioned a major general in the

---

[5] Now Winslow, Maine.
[6] Goold, *Portland in the Past,* 369-70.

Maine militia. He lived and practiced law at the Fort Western settlement in Hallowell, and was twice elected a senator to the Massachusetts Legislature.

William Lithgow, Jr., was 39 when he prosecuted Bird and Hanson in 1790. Two years earlier he served as defense attorney for John O'Neil who was charged with the murder of Michael Cleary for money at Pemaquid Falls. O'Neil was convicted and his hanging on September 4, 1788, was recorded as the first judicial execution on the Kennebec River. After Bird's conviction it would be said that those charged with murder didn't want Lithgow involved in the case either for or against them.

About five years after his appointment to serve as the first U.S. District Attorney for the District of Maine, he resigned from his duties and surrendered his military commission due to illness. On February 16, 1796, at the age of 46, he died of liver disease. Lithgow never married, but at the time of his death he was engaged to Mary Deering of Portland, who later became the wife of Commodore Edward Preble, also of Portland. It was said that he "was esteemed a good lawyer; he was eloquent and forcible in his forensic efforts, and was remarkable for his noble figure, manly beauty and accomplished manners." [7]

---

[7] Except as otherwise noted, all biographical information on William Lithgow, Jr., Esq., taken from Nathan Goold, *Falmouth Neck in the Revolution* (Portland, Maine: Thurston Press, 1897), 40; James W. North, *The History of Augusta, Maine: A facsimile of the 1870 edition with a new foreword by Edwin A. Churchill* (Somersworth, NH: New England History Press, 1981), 224-25; Charles Elventon Nash, *The*

JOHN FROTHINGHAM, ESQ.

(1750 – 1826)

DEFENSE ATTORNEY

John Frothingham was born in Charlestown, Massachusetts, on September 29, 1750, a son of Deacon John and Esther (Call) Frothingham. He studied at Dummer Academy and graduated at Harvard College in 1771. After teaching for several years at Exeter and Greenland in New Hampshire, in 1774 he moved to Portland, Maine, to take a position as schoolmaster and, when not teaching, studied law under Theophilus Bradbury who was eleven years senior to Frothingham, also a Harvard alumnus, and the first educated lawyer to settle in Portland.

Though admitted to practice law at the Cumberland Bar in March of 1779, Frothingham did not abandon his vocation as a teacher, which was probably more profitable than his legal work. In 1780, he was appointed Cumberland County

---

History of Augusta: First Settlements and Early Days as a Town Including the Diary of Mrs. Martha Moore Ballard (1785 to 1812) (Augusta, ME: Charles E. Nash & Son, 1904), 272-73; and Willis, *A History of the Law*, 105-06.

Attorney, and was collector of the excise for Maine. He married Patty May of Boston in 1784 and two years later he was elected to serve as representative to the General Court. He was 40 years of age when assigned by the court to defend Thomas Bird and Hans Hanson.

Mr. Frothingham was clerk of the First Parish Church for 34 years, Register of Probate for 12 years, and judge of the Court of Common Pleas for eight years. In the latter part of his life he lost his sight, and he died February 8, 1826, at age 76. John and Patty Frothingham had a large family, but only four of their children survived him. It was said that he was "a faithful, upright, intelligent, and honest man".[8]

---

[8] Biographical information on John Frothingham, Esq., taken from Willis, *A History of the Law,* 103-04, 675; Willis, *The History of Portland,* fn 625; and Clifford K. Shipton, *Sibley's Harvard Graduates, Vol. XVII 1768-1771: Biographical Sketches of Those Who Attended Harvard College in the Classes 1667-1771 with Bibliographical and Other Notes* (Boston: Massachusetts Historical Society, 1975), 520-21.

WILLIAM SYMMES, ESQ.

(1760 – 1807)

DEFENSE ATTORNEY

William Symmes was born May 26, 1760, at Andover, Massachusetts, the eldest son of Rev. Dr. William Symmes and his wife Anna (Gee), who died twelve years later. He graduated at Harvard College in 1780, and spent some time as a private tutor in Virginia where he met "a pure African" who became his mistress. We do not know if this woman was a slave, but if she was, it would have been necessary for Symmes to have either purchased her freedom or *stolen* her from her so-called *rightful owner*. In any case, she was with Symmes when he later returned to Andover.[9] Following his return he read law with Theophilus Bradbury for the required period and was admitted to the Essex (County, Massachusetts) Bar.

Symmes was recognized as a most competent attorney and his peers took special notice of the fact that he stood in opposition to the new constitution then being considered by the states. A majority in Andover thought likewise and Symmes was elected to represent them at the

---

[9] *"Hawthorne"*, The New York Times, June 7, 1902.

Massachusetts Constitutional Convention. During the debate, however, Symmes changed his mind and, voting in favor of adoption, ended his remarks by saying "I recall my former opposition, such as it was, to this Constitution, and shall—especially as the amendments are a standing instruction to our delegates until they are obtained—give it my unreserved assent. In so doing, I stand acquitted to my own conscience; I hope and trust I shall to my constituents, and [*laying his hand on his breast*] I know I shall before God."

He learned in subsequent weeks and months that the hope and trust he assigned to his constituents had been misplaced. They were so angry by his perceived betrayal and made his life so uncomfortable that within two years, in 1790, he moved to Portland, Maine, and established a successful law practice there. He was but 28 years of age when he was assigned by the court to defend Thomas Bird and Hans Hanson. It was perhaps the arrogance of youth that prompted him to disparage District Attorney William Lithgow's credentials in open court, noting that Lithgow was not a college graduate. However, Symmes may have merely been engaging in a bit of professional jousting, for which he was well known, to unnerve his opponent during the trial.

William Freeman, one of Symmes' students, said "(t)he personal appearance of Mr. Symmes was stately and dignified. He was, in all respects, a gentleman in his manners, and emphatically one of the old school. He was affable and polite, and commanded affection as well as respect. He may truly be said to have been one of the most imposing and influential men at that time in Portland." But Freeman also noted that a cloud was cast upon Symmes latter days by the use of intoxicating drinks. "Often, when mellow with brandy, his favorite drink, he was brilliant, and threw more light on a subject under discussion than any other speaker."

On one occasion, Symmes made a motion to Judge Thacher's court, which he was zealously arguing and growing increasingly more impatient with the judge's frequent interruptions. Judge Thacher finally said, "Mr. Symmes, you need not persist in arguing the point, for I am not a court of errors, and cannot give a final judgment." "I know," replied Symmes, "that you can't give a final judgment, but as to your not being a *court of errors*, I will not say."[10]

Symmes never married, but in 1805 his African mistress presented him with a mulatto son who would bear his

---

[10] Except as otherwise noted, all biographical information on William Symmes taken from *Life in a New England Town 1787, 1788. Diary of John Quincy Adams while a student in the office of Theophilus Parsons at Newburyport* (Boston: Little, Brown, and Company, 1903), 38; Sarah Loring Bailey, *Historical Sketches of Andover (Comprising the Present Towns of North Andover and Andover) Massachusetts* (Boston: Houghton, Mifflin and Company, 1880), 449; "Elliot's Debates, Volume II", TeachingAmericanHistory.org http://www.teachingamericanhistory.org/ ratification/elliot/vol2/ massachusetts0206.html (Accessed November 10, 2008); and Willis, *A History of the Law*, 675.

father's name. Whether the boy's mother survived childbirth is not known, but two years later, on January 14, 1807, the boy's father, William Symmes, Esq., died at age 45. Four months later the boy's grandfather, the Rev. Dr. William Symmes (1728-1807), also died. Samuel Fessenden, one of William Symmes' colleagues at the Cumberland Bar, placed the child with Captain Jonathan Britton of Otisfield, Maine, to be raised.[11]

William Symmes (1805-1871) grew up in Otisfield spending much of his youth hunting, fishing, and exploring Maine's Sebago Lake region with his boyhood friend Nathaniel Hawthorne of literary fame who lived in nearby Raymond. At age 20, William became a seaman, and later, during and after the Civil War, he was a detective employed by Colonel Lafayette C. Baker's infamous detective agency in Washington, D.C.[12] He died in Pensacola, Florida, on October 28, 1871, at the age of 66.[13]

---

[11] *"Hawthorne"*, The New York Times, June 7, 1902.
[12] Samuel T. Pickard, *Hawthorne's First Diary* (Boston: Houghton, Mifflin, 1897), 42.
[13] Ibid, 26.

Henry Dearborn, M.D.

(1751 – 1829)

U.S. Marshal

for the District of Maine

Henry Dearborn was born in North Hampton, New Hampshire, on February 23, 1751, son of Simon and Sarah Dearborn, and received an excellent education before studying medicine under the tutelage of Dr. Hall Jackson of Portsmouth, New Hampshire. He married first in 1771 to Mary Bartlett; second in 1780 to the widow Dorcas (Osgood) Marble, with whom he had a daughter and a son; and third in 1813 to the widow Sarah Bowdoin.

Three years before the American Revolution began Dr. Dearborn opened a medical practice at Nottingham-Square, New Hampshire. He organized a militia company, to which he was elected captain, and spent his leisure time in military exercises convinced that the liberties of his homeland would eventually have to be surrendered or defended. "On the morning of April 20, 1775, receiving notice of battle at Lexington, he and 60 others assembled and struck out for Cambridge, 55 miles away, which they reached in less than 24 hours."

In the fall and winter of that year Captain Dearborn accompanied Benedict Arnold's ill-fated expedition to Quebec. The expedition soon outdistanced their supply line and the men were suffering so severely from the cold and hunger that Dearborn offered one contingent his favorite dog, which they divided among themselves. He led his company in the assault at Quebec on December 31, 1775, and was taken prisoner. The British paroled Dearborn in May, 1776, and exchanged him for British prisoners the following March. Ten days later he was promoted to the rank of major.

He held commands at Bunker Hill, Brandywine, Stillwater, Germantown, Bemis Heights, Saratoga, Valley Forge, and Monmouth, and was at the siege of Yorktown when Lord Cornwallis and his army were captured. In 1781, he was promoted to the rank of colonel and remained in the army until the peace of 1783. He moved to Monmouth, Maine, in 1784, and three years later was appointed a major general in the Maine militia. General Dearborn was 38 when President George Washington appointed him to serve as U.S. Marshall for the District of Maine, and 39 when he carried out the execution of Thomas Bird.

He was elected to the U.S. House of Representatives in 1793 and held his seat until 1797. President Thomas Jefferson appointed him Secretary of War in 1801. At the conclusion of Jefferson's two terms, Dearborn accepted an appointment to serve as collector of the port at Boston.

During the war of 1812, President James Madison gave Dearborn command of military operations in the northeast, but he had little experience commanding large numbers of troops and his invasion of Canada ended in defeat. He was relieved of his command on July 6, 1813, and President Madison nominated him to his former post as Secretary of War, but there was such public protest that the nomination was withdrawn and Dearborn retired to Massachusetts. He later served as Minister to Portugal for two years, and then took up retirement once again in Roxbury, Massachusetts. On June 6, 1829, Henry Dearborn died at the age of 78. He has been described as "a man of full stature and of dignified and commanding personal appearance; he was noted for decision in action and rigidity in discipline." [14]

---

[14] All biographical information on Henry Dearborn taken from George Thomas Little, A.M., Litt. D., ed., *Genealogical and Family History of the State of Maine,* Vol. II, (New York: Lewis Historical Publ. Co., 1909); Wilbur D. Spencer, *Maine Immortals: Including Many Unique Characters in Early Maine History,* (Augusta, ME: Northeastern Press, 1932); and William H. Smith, Esq., *"General Henry Dearborn. A Genealogical Sketch."* The Maine Historical and Genealogical Recorder, Vol. III (Portland, Maine: S.M. Watson, Publ., 1886).

Henry Sewall

(1752 – 1845)

Clerk of the U.S. District Court

District of Maine

Henry Sewall was born in York, Maine, on October 24, 1752. He was raised on his father's farm and little is known of his education except that it was well accepted and practiced for he had a beautiful and graceful hand and a masterful command of words whether written or spoken. He was 23 when war broke out with Great Britain and he enlisted in the army as a private. Through the course of the war he rose to the rank of captain of infantry having fought at Ticonderoga and Saratoga, and later joining the main army under General Washington at Pennsylvania, wintering at Valley Forge.

After the war he settled at Fort Western, Maine, and became a merchant. In 1788, he went to New York and opened an office for the buying and selling of public securities, but this enterprise failed and he returned to Maine, living in Hallowell and Augusta for many years. When the Maine militia was formed he was commissioned a colonel in the 8th Division under Maj. Gen. William Lithgow, Jr. On the same day that Judge David Sewall was administered the oath of office to serve as U.S. District Court Judge, Judge Sewall appointed his cousin, Henry Sewall, then 37, to serve as Clerk of the District Court of Maine, a post he held for 29 years.

Following the death of General William Lithgow, Jr., General Henry Dearborn was assigned to command that division and Colonel Henry Sewall was promoted to brigadier general. Subsequently, when General Dearborn was appointed to serve as Secretary of War in 1801, General Henry Sewall succeeded him in the command of the division.

> General Sewall was strictly and thoroughly an upright, conscientious, and religious man: when he took office, and he did not accept any that he was not competent to fill, he had no other purpose than to discharge the duties with a single view to their true objects and ends; he was faithful to the letter; he neglected nothing that belonged to the station, whether civil or military, whether in detail or a general principle; and when he retired from them, it was with a clear, unclouded retrospect of unequivocal endeavor to perform his entire duty to every intent.

He was a large man with strong features and a military bearing, especially when mounted on a steed. One his aids presented him with a noble white charger upon which he made "an imposing and spirited figure, but as he had short bow-legs he did not appear to so good advantage on foot." During his long life he took three wives. The first, in 1786, was Tabitha Sewall of Georgetown, a cousin, with whom he had seven children; the second, in 1811, was Rachel Crosby of Salem, also a cousin; and the third, in 1833, was Elizabeth Lowell of Boston, who survived him. Henry Sewall died on September 4, 1845, just seven weeks before his 93rd birthday.[15]

---

[15] All biographical information on Henry Sewall taken from Willis, *A History of the Law*, 671-76; and North, *The History of Augusta*, 226-28.

John Waite

(1732-1820)

Cumberland County Sheriff

John Waite was born in Newbury, Massachusetts, in July of 1732. Six years later, his family moved to Portland. He began his adult life as a mariner and was captain of the schooner *Jolly Philip* engaged in the expedition to the Bay of Fundy in 1755, memorialized in Henry Wadsworth Longfellow's poem *Evangeline*, when he was ordered to remove Acadians from Nova Scotia and carry them to Georgia. Two years later he commanded the sloop *Swallow* in the ill-fated expedition to Louisburg, and in 1759 he commanded the same vessel in the expedition to Quebec. He witnessed the Battle of the Plains of Abraham from the deck of the *Swallow*, and wrote an account of Major General James Wolfe's death during that assault. Earlier that year, on January 15, he married his wife Hannah with whom he had 13 children; the youngest born in 1783.

He was very active in town affairs, but pursued a life at sea until the onset of the American Revolution when he was appointed Sheriff of Cumberland County. His predecessor, William Tyng, joined the Royalists in 1775 and fled the country. That same year John Waite was promoted to colonel of the First Regiment, looking after the defenses of Portland and providing for those who suffered when the town was burned by the British. Waite was 57 when Jackson, Bird, and Hanson were placed in his custody.

He made a "venerable figure . . . still erect, of medium height and rather broad, crowned with a three-cornered cocked hat of the Revolutionary model, blue coat with bright buttons, a buff vest, and a sword by his side; his countenance grave, not to say stern, as he seemed to the juvenile mind, which associated harsh duties with his office; heavy, overhanging eyebrows, and his white staff, the badge of his office, in hand, had an imposing effect upon all spectators, old as well as young."

In 1809, at the age of 77, John Waite resigned as the county's sheriff having held the office for 34 years. In his letter of resignation he lamented, "Infirmity incident to old age is the lot of man; it creeps upon us insensibly". He died in 1820 at the age of 88.[16]

---

[16] All biographical information on Sheriff John Waite taken from Willis, *A History of The Law; Goold, Portland in the Past;* and Goold, *A History of Peaks Island and its People.*

Nathaniel Fadre Fosdick

(1760-1819)

Naval Officer

and

Collector of Customs

Port of Portland, Maine

Nathaniel Fasdre Fosdick was born in Marblehead, Massachusetts, on September 14, 1760. He graduated at Harvard College in 1779, and moved to Portland after the war to pursue commercial interests. He married Abigail, a daughter of Ephraim and Mary Jones, on September 5, 1784. When Thomas Child, the previous naval officer and collector, died in January of 1788, Nathanial Deering notified Fosdick that same night and urged him to move quickly. Fosdick immediately left for Boston, riding on horseback in the middle of a violent snow storm to secure the post for himself, which proved advantageous, for his competitors' horses were not saddled until the next day.[17]

---

[17]   Willis, *History of Portland,* 462.

In 1789, when the sloop *Mary* was captured off the coast of Maine, he had held his post little more than a year. At this time he was 28 years of age and lived in Portland with his wife and three children. Fosdick was removed from his position in 1802 by the Jefferson administration and he later moved to Salem, Massachusetts, where he died of dropsy[18] on September 13, 1819, the day before his 59th birthday. His wife died in Boston on April 5, 1851, at age 91.[19]

---

[18] Edema or swelling of the body usually caused by congestive heart failure or kidney disease.

[19] Except as otherwise noted, all biographical information on Nathaniel Fadre Fosdick taken from Joseph Crook Anderson II, ed., Maine Families in 1790, Vol. 8, Maine Genealogical Society Special Publication No. 42 (Rockport, Maine: Picton Press, 2003), 157-58.

Thomas Motley

Cumberland County Jailer

Thomas Motley was the son of John Motley who immigrated to Portland from Belfast, Ireland, in 1738 and married Mary Roberts the same year. Thomas married Sheriff John Waite's sister, Emma, who was 14 years younger than her brother. The Motleys had seven sons: Robert, Richard, George, Henry, Thomas Jr., Edward, and the youngest, Charles, who was born in 1785. [20]

Motley was the jailer (1781-1793) when Bird and Hanson were held here. He and his family lived in and managed a public house, which "was called 'Freemason's Arms' and had a swinging sign in front, inscribed with a representation of the square and compasses."[21]

---

[20] Willis, *History of Portland,* 823.

[21] Goold, *Portland in the Past,* 496-97.

Portland, Maine
1789-90

PORTLAND 1789-90

The peninsula of land we know as Portland, Maine, referred to by English colonists and early Americans simply as The Neck until late in the 19th century, was separated from the town of Falmouth by the Massachusetts Legislature on July 4, 1786. There was talk, at that time, of separating the entire District of Maine from Massachusetts, but that would not happen for another 34 years.

The Neck's new name, Portland, was one of three considered, including *Casco* and *Falmouthport*, but a majority favored *Portland* due to its euphonious sound and the fact that it was the earliest English name applied to a nearby island and the opposite mainland,[87] which are separated by a channel called Portland Sound. The headland on which a lighthouse has stood since 1791 has always been known as Portland Head.[88]

In 1790, the proposed Portland Head Light tower stood 58 feet high, but at that height the light would not be visible to vessels approaching from the south. It was calculated that another 29 feet would have to be added, including the lantern[*], but funds designated for the project were depleted. In August of that year Congress appropriated $1,500.00 to complete the work and it was finally lighted on January 10, 1791.[89]

---

[*] It was later determined that this would be too high and 20 feet of the finished height was removed.

The Portland peninsula was roughly three miles long and a mile wide. Bramhall Hill at the west end, named for its first English occupant who took possession in 1698,[90] rose 175 feet; the lowest point near the center of the peninsula was but 57 feet, and the summit of Munjoy Hill at the east end, named for its first English occupant who took possession in 1659,[91] was 161 feet above sea level.[92] A silhouette of its southern elevation appeared very much like that of a western saddle. Toward the east or forward end of the saddle seat, on the inner side of the swell, a great pine rose from the southwest corner of Portland's Eastern Cemetery, and it could be seen by mariners from many miles off; a welcome landmark to navigators seeking anchorage at Portland Harbor.[93]

The first United States Census was compiled in 1790 and, at that time, Portland was the residence of 366 families consisting of 564 free white males 16-years-of-age or older, 537 free white males under the age of 16 years, 1,123 free white females, and 16 people classified only as "other free persons", for a total of 2,240.[94] Presumably most or all of these other free persons were of African-American heritage. Slavery was abolished in Massachusetts, including the District of Maine, in 1783.

In addition to those of English and African heritage, there were several families of Scotch-Irish ancestry, rigid Presbyterians, whose forebears arrived in the autumn of 1718 from Ireland in a vessel carrying 20 families. They suffered severely that winter for their provisions were inadequate to sustain them and the stores of the inhabitants were insufficient as well. In December the General Court was petitioned for relief and "one hundred bushels of Indian meal" was allowed "for the poor Irish people".

In the spring, most of these families sailed to Newburyport and later established the town of Londonderry in what is now New Hampshire, but was then part of Massachusetts.[95] However, several families remained including the Armstrongs, Means, Jamesons, Gyles, Simontons, and McDonalds.[96]

More than 1,000 Acadians, or Neutral French, were brought from Nova Scotia to Massachusetts in 1755 and distributed among different towns to be supported. A number of these were assigned to the town of Falmouth, which then included The Neck, but whether any of these remained is uncertain.[*]

Four years earlier there were but one or two brigs of less than 200 tons in Portland Harbor owned by local residents and engaged in the West India trade, and several locally owned schooners and sloops of very small tonnage employed in the coastal trade. These numbers progressively increased during the following eight years to 11,000 tons consisting of 13 ships, 24 brigs, 23 schooners,

---

[*] A result of the Great Upheaval or Deportation ordered by the British and immortalized by Henry Wadsworth Longfellow in his poem "Evangeline".

and 20 sloops. Most of these carried lumber – principally large pine trees hewed square, called "ton timber" – to Europe and ports along the eastern coast of the United States.[97]

Many, if not most, of the adult male residents of Portland in 1790 were shipbuilders or seamen. Others were tanners, distillers, rope makers, chandlers, soap makers, blacksmiths, loggers, sawyers, farmers, and longshoremen. There were as well merchants whose stores were kept by their wives, as was the custom; a newspaper owned by Thomas B. Waite; at least three physicians, Drs. Nathaniel Coffin, Jr., John Lowther, and Shirley Erving, all of whom studied at hospitals in London; and five practicing lawyers including Daniel Davis, John Frothingham, Salmon Chase, Samuel Cooper Johonnot, and William Symmes.

In 1789 the voters supported a motion "to have two schoolmasters, one for each end of the town". The following year the school committee required the teachers to shift from one school to the other every day, "alternating their services and giving nobody cause to complain that one part of the town was better served than the other."[98]

There were at least four separate religious groups and three ordained ministers, though two of these preached in the same church. The Reverends Thomas Smith and Samuel Deane were co-pastors of the First Church, which adhered to the Congregational order. Rev. Smith arrived in 1725 and was the first pastor of this the first organized church on The Neck.[99] Rev. Deane was called in 1764 to assist the aging Rev. Smith.[100]

St. Paul's Episcopal Church had no ordained minister since the early days of the Revolutionary War when its pastor, Rev. John Wiswell, a Tory, departed for England. Mr. Edward Oxnard, a graduate of Harvard and a Loyalist who fled to England during the war, but returned in 1785, served as lay-reader. St. Paul's was founded by individuals who had seceded from the First Church in 1764.[101]

The Rev. Elijah Kellog served as pastor of the Second Church whose members had seceded from the First Church in 1787.[102] And finally, the fourth and smallest group was of the Quaker covenant, which according to tradition had no ordained minister. In 1790 they were first granted permission to hold a separate meeting for worship at the home of William Purington on Church Lane, which extended northward from Middle Street between Pearl and Fiddle Lane*.[103]

The King's Highway

The overland journey between Portsmouth, New Hampshire, and Portland, Maine, circa 1789-90, was long and arduous. Most travelers likely preferred to sail by coastal packet for time and comfort's sake, but for those

---

* Now Franklin Street.

who dared not suffer the often troubled sea, the alternatives were few. Points east of Boston received no regularly scheduled mail until 1760, when Benjamin Franklin was appointed Colonial Postmaster. But in that year, for the first time, Franklin established weekly mail service from Boston to Portland, and the newly completed Upper King's Highway from Kittery to Portland thereafter became known as the Post Road. Later, George Washington ordered the placement of 129 large granite blocks between Boston and Portland at one mile intervals to serve as milestones. In 1953, one of these, in Wells, bearing the inscription "B 89 1769", could still be found, though it had sunk deep into the ground. [104]

Some two decades after regular mail service had begun an enterprising entrepreneur who was serving as post rider between Portsmouth and Portland in 1787, Joseph Barnard of Kennebunk, took to riding a wagon drawn by a team of horses. The wagon was of the buckboard type, crude and uncomfortable; the passenger seats had no backs to lean against, nor protection from the heat and dust in summer or the driving snow and bitter cold in winter.

Mr. Barnard advertised his service in Portland's Cumberland Gazette, advising "Those Ladies and Gentlemen who choose the expeditious, cheap, and commodious way of stage traveling . . ." to leave their names at Motley's Tavern. He made the round trip once weekly, weather permitting, leaving Portland on Saturday morning, arriving in Portsmouth Monday evening, and departing on his return trip to Portland each Tuesday.[105]

Stroudwater

Approaching Portland, before the turnpike was built across the Scarborough Marshes in 1800, the highway took a devious route between Dunstan and Stroudwater with a difficult climb over Scottow's Hill. Depending on the weather and the time of day, Barnard might have stopped at Broad's Tavern, which rested in the shade of a giant oak tree on the site of what is now the Portland International Jetport. Thaddeus Broad's tavern was the most modern hostelry and eatery east of Boston. Renowned as Maine's first and most successful inn during the period between the Revolution and the Civil War, it boasted of having catered to such prominent figures as Lafayette and President James Monroe. In later years, when Mr. Broad's son, Silas, took over as host, he chained a black bear to the oak tree as an added attraction.

Bramhall Hill

Finally, Barnard's team pulled its master, wagon, and payload over the two wooden bridges that spanned the Stroudwater and Fore Rivers, and up a steep incline to the top of Bramhall Hill, which was also known as Haggett's Hill.[106] George Bramhall's farm of 350 acres was entirely fenced in and embraced all of the land bounded by what is now Congress and Vaughn Streets, including the site of the Maine Medical Center complex and the entire Western Promenade. His house stood in the vicinity of the ramps to the Casco Bay Bridge, at the end of what is now Danforth Street. Atop Bramhall's Hill, evening travelers passed through the shadow of a gallows built in 1772 for the execution of one Goodwin who was convicted of murdering a man by throwing him from a boat into Casco Bay. Thomas Bird was hung from the same gallows in 1790.

Beyond Bramhall's farm, if a west or south wind was blowing, one was greeted by the pungent aroma of what was called "Hog Town", where the townspeople allowed their pigs to roam and root freely within a fenced and stonewalled area now bounded by Spring and Brackett Streets. If the prevailing winds were from the east, however, the smell was every inbound travelers' welcome at the very instant that they crested Bramhall's Hill. Further eastward, between "Hog Town" and the town boundary, approximately along the line of what is now High Street running from north to south, there was little to see other than swampland and several frog ponds.

Riding about the streets and lanes of Portland in 1790, it would not have been at all unusual to have seen one or more of the 30 or 40 two-wheeled horse-drawn chaises then gaining in popularity among the wealthier folks who could afford them. The gentlemen of these successful families, such as the Tates, Prebles, Wadsworths, and Deerings, were often seen in fair weather, reins and whip in hand, raising a cloud of dust as they dashed about the peninsula tending to their businesses. In rare leisure moments, they wore cocked hats, red cloaks, and powdered wigs, and were frequently attended by a slave in livery. Some of the men wore full-length pantaloons as Captain Joseph Titcomb had by then introduced them to Portland after returning from the West Indies wearing the latest in men's fashion himself.

Portland was still recovering from English Naval Captain Henry Mowatt's attack when most of the town was burned to the ground in 1775. Few had dared to rebuild until the war was formally ended with the Treaty of Paris in 1883, and many naked chimneys still stood as monuments to the devastation, particularly along the waterfront, Middle, and King (now India) Streets where most of the local industries and business houses were located. Rebuilding was "considered a hazardous undertaking, considering the disturbed state of the colonies, and the exposed condition of the town." [107]

The Waterfront

Joseph Ingraham, a silversmith, was one of the exceptions and the first to rebuild on the same site in 1777. It was a narrow, two-story house with his silversmith shop in one side on the corner of Fore Street and Fish Lane (now Exchange Street) opposite Long Wharf. Here, along the waterfront, before it was filled in to accommodate Commercial Street, skilled Negro stevedores had taken over the wharves. The principal article of export was "ton timber", which was exported to England. Manufactured lumber was not admitted to English ports as a means of protecting the labor of their own sawyers. In addition to lumber, soap, candles, and dried codfish were consigned to the captain who sold his secondary cargo to the highest bidder and bought another of sugar, molasses and rum, which he brought back to Portland.

Clay Cove, at the foot of King Street, was for the most part occupied by Nathaniel Deering's shipbuilding business. Other businesses on the waterfront included a tannery, a distillery, and Benjamin Titcomb's blacksmith shop. On Thames Street, just east of Clay Cove, the widow of Brigadier Jedediah Preble built a mansion in 1786. The same year, Benjamin Woodman built Portland's second brick home at the corner of Fore and Silver Streets.

British Captain Henry Mowatt's Attack

Clay Cove was also the site where Captain Mowatt's forces landed during the burning of Portland on October 18, 1775. Though four British vessels had begun firing a cascade of flaming carcasses,[22] bombs, and shells at the town at 9:40 in the morning, they had little effect during the first few hours of the attack. Uncooperative winds and the determination of inhabitants to extinguish the flames prevented them from spreading to Mowatt's satisfaction. Several landing parties consisting of 30 British seamen and marines under the command of Lieutenant Frasier landed at 3:00 that afternoon. Meeting with little resistance, Frasier ordered his men to enter the town where they threw torches into the doors and windows of the homes and shops that were not yet burning. Most of the townspeople were frantically engaged in evacuating their families and attempting to move their belongings to safety, but some advanced to meet the marauders and fired on them, wounding two of them. By 4:00 P.M., the British landing party returned to the flotilla.

The spreading of flames from the structures ignited by the landing party, the continuing bombardment, and changing winds converged into a great conflagration and by

---

[22] Hollow iron cases filled with combustibles. Flames issued through holes pierced in the sides.

sundown Mowatt ordered the firing to cease. When the British flotilla weighed anchor and left the harbor, Portland was engulfed by flame. The lower and most densely developed end of town was completely destroyed.[108] In all, 414 structures were reduced to ashes, including 136 homes.[109]

Middle Street

The home of Thomas Cummings, which stood on the north corner of King and Middle Streets, destroyed during Mowatt's attack, had also been rebuilt on the same site. Cummings operated a store within his house and carried on a brisk business selling dry goods including beaver hats and fashionable clothing.

Two churches stood on Middle Street, the Second Parish on the south side at the corner of Deer Street, and nearly opposite that St. Paul's Episcopal at the corner of Church Street. St. Paul's had a tower with a bell. The Second Parish had no tower but a flagstaff was erected so Sexton Burns could give notice of services by hoisting a flag. There was some degree of hostility between Sexton Fernald of St. Paul's, who was a Tory during the war, and Sexton Burns, who took great pleasure in flaunting his flag in Fernald's sight. In response, Fernald took great pleasure in tolling his bell with as much vigor as he could muster. It was said, we suspect by a member of the Second Parish, that one Sunday after ringing his bell, Fernald crossed Middle Street and asked Burns "What do you hoist that flag for?" Burns angrily but wittily replied, "To let people know when your bell rings."

The post office was kept at the home and office of Judge Samuel Freeman on Middle Street between St. Paul's Church and Fiddle Lane (now Franklin Arterial). Judge Freeman was appointed Postmaster of Portland on October 1, 1775, by none other than Postmaster General Benjamin Franklin.

Greenwood's Tavern was on the south corner of Middle and Silver Streets. It was three stories with windowless brick ends and when built in 1774 was one of the first partially brick homes on The Neck. Joseph Jewett bought the building in 1783 and kept a store in the lower eastern room.

Further west, Joshua Freeman's Tavern stood on the corner of Middle and Fish (now Exchange) Streets. Though Portland boasted many public taverns or so-called houses of entertainment, dancing was not considered an acceptable expression of joyful fun. Years earlier, Theophilus Bradbury, a lawyer, and his wife, Sarah; Nathaniel Deering, a shipbuilder, and his wife, Dorcas; and John Waite, a ship's captain and later the Sheriff of Cumberland County, and his wife, Hannah; and several other couples were indicted for dancing here in December of 1765. Mr. Bradbury pleaded that the room where the couples danced had been hired for a holiday celebration and was not to be considered a public place. The court sustained his plea.

Near the west end of Middle Street, on the south side, Dr. Shirley Erving, a physician, maintained an office and an apothecary. Here he sold drugs, medicines, groceries, dye stuffs, and "An assortment of WINES and SPIRITS, free from adulteration, consisting of Maderia, Sherry, Lisbon, Malaga, Teneriffe and Claret Wines – French Brandy, Jamaica Spirits, Westindia and Newengland Rum: all of which he will sell on the most reasonable terms." [110]

Beyond Dr. Erving's establishment to the west were two very popular public houses. One was Marston's Tavern, a two-story wooden structure with a hip roof, which also stood on the south side of Middle Street. Here Captain Henry Mowatt was briefly held prisoner in May of 1775, five months before he returned to destroy the town. The other was Freemason's Arms, which was operated by the county jailer, Thomas Motley, and his wife, Emma, with assistance from several of the eldest of their seven sons.

Haymarket Square

The west end of Middle Street spilled into Haymarket Square (now Monument Square) where the masters of merchant ships and other businessmen traded rum, molasses, salt, iron, and manufactures for lumber and country produce. Here Arthur Savage erected a "hay machine"[111] capable of weighing up to three tons; a wagonload of hay was raised from overhead by a lever purchase connected to the wagon's wheels by chains.

Directly opposite the hay market were the offices of Thomas B. Wait, editor and publisher of The Cumberland Gazette. And on the site where the Soldiers and Sailors Monument now stands, there was an old blockhouse built in 1746 for the common defense during the Indian Wars. In 1753 a lean-to was added to the blockhouse, presumably divided into prison cells, that was "thirty-five feet long, fifteen wide and seven stud, with one stack of chimneys of four smokers. The building is to be of good, square, sound, hewed or sawed timber, well boarded, clapboarded and shingled outside, with lining inside of good, sound oak plank, spiked on". [112] Hans Hanson and Thomas Bird were held here from July 22, 1789, to June 5 and June 25, 1790, respectively.

It was not uncommon for those frequenting the square to find themselves dodging stones thrown by Billy Hans, a veteran of the Revolution who had fought at Stillwater, Saratoga, Monmouth, Quaker Hill, and Yorktown, and had survived the wretched winter of 1777-78 at Valley Forge. Billy was generally very well natured, but he made his reverence for George Washington well known and on otherwise boring days, when the local children had nothing better to do, they would cast doubt on the general's courage under fire by proclaiming in Billy's presence "Washington got behind a stump". This agitated Billy so, especially when he was drinking, that he would hurl stones at them, some of which went astray and threatened innocent bystanders. [113]

Back Street

On Back (now Congress) Street, west of Haymarket Square, the White Horse Tavern stood at the corner of Beaver (now Brown) Street. It was built in 1785 by Captain Ebenezer Davis who always wore the cocked hat and small clothes of the old school. The widow Bethia Rollins and her four children also lived in a house at this intersection. On April 4, 1783, Samuel Rollins, 40, had been killed by the bursting of a cannon fired by townspeople who were rejoicing at news that a peace with England had finally been concluded just four days earlier.

General Peleg Wadsworth lived within a block west of Haymarket Square in the first brick home to be built in Portland. Begun in 1785 using bricks imported from Philadelphia, the plan called for 16-inch-thick walls, but it was soon determined that the builders had miscalculated and another lot of bricks had to be ordered. When the house was completed in 1786, it was two stories high with four chimneys and a fireplace in every room.

Though now in the heart of the city, the house when built was on the outskirts of the town, amid green fields, and commanding fine views of the ocean, which it faced, and of the mountains and forests away toward the western horizon. Built in the old colonial style, with the hall running through the centre, there is still an air of old-time hospitality about it as one steps in from the street and faces the broad stairway.

The interior is but little changed, for though repairs have been needed on so old a building, care has been taken to preserve as nearly as possible the original appearance of the rooms. All the windows have the same old panelled wooden shutters, as of yore, and some of those on the back of the house retain the old casements, with their many tiny panes of glass; the doors all have their curious old "box latches," and thanks to the generous thickness of the walls, there are wide windowseats in all of the lower rooms, cushioned and inviting. On the left, upon entering, is the parlor, which, at the time the house was built, was the largest private reception room in Portland, and in this room was placed the first piano to be brought to town. It was probably a spinet, and the story is told that such was the curiosity of the country people regarding this wonder, that they would stand around the windows looking in and listening whenever the instrument was being played, and even offer money to have the music continued.

When the Wadsworth family moved in there were six children, one of whom, Zilpah, the future mother of the poet, was a little maid of seven or eight. Here in 1790 was born another son, Alexander Scammel, named for General Scammel, a friend and college classmate of Wadsworth, and the man for whom also one of the forts in Portland Harbor was named. [114]

Immediately to the right, Wadsworth built a two-story wooden structure in which he operated a store.

General Wadsworth was, after General Solomon Lovell, second-in-command of land forces during the ill-fated Penobscot Expedition in 1779, which resulted in the loss of more than 40 vessels, most of which ran aground and were burned in the Penobscot River to prevent them from being captured by the British. Commodore Dudley Saltonstall of Massachusetts, who commanded the expedition, was later court-martialed and convicted of failing to engage the enemy and was dismissed from military service. Lt. Colonel Paul Revere, also of Massachusetts and commander of an artillery unit, was accused of insubordination and cowardice but he later had the charges cleared.

Following his retirement from military service, General Wadsworth operated a mercantile store and was the first to be elected Representative to Congress from this district. His daughter, Zilpah, and son-in-law, Stephen Longfellow, Esq., were the parents of the renowned poet Henry Wadsworth Longfellow.

To the east, just beyond Haymarket Square, was the home of Rev. Samuel Deane; a two-story wooden structure with three dormer windows on the second floor-front. He was pastor of the First Parish Church and came to Portland in 1764 to assist and eventually succeed Rev. Dr. Thomas Smith. Rev. Deane was a graduate of Harvard College (1760) and, in addition to his pastoral duties, devoted himself to agricultural experiments and pursuits. His home was surrounded by gardens and orchards that extended northward carpeting the hillside down to Back Cove. In 1790, he published his *Georgical Dictionary, or New England Farmer,* the first encyclopedia of agriculture published in America. It remained the standard in New England for many years. When Brown University honored him with an advanced degree that same year, it was suggested that "since it could not have been for his theology, it must have been for his agricultural fame."[115] Rev. Deane married Eunice, a daughter of Moses Pearson, in 1766, but they had no children.

Next along Back Street, on the site where the Universalist-Unitarian Church now stands, was the First Parish Meeting House, affectionately referred to by townspeople as *Old Jerusalem.* It was built in 1740 and the congregation gathered to worship in this building for the first time on

July 20 of the same year, but it was not as large then, nor did it have a tower or steeple. Eighteen years later, Captain Alexander Ross returned from England with an 800 pound bell that was suspended from a frame outside the building. The next year, in 1759, frugality succumbed to overcrowding and the structure was sawn through on both sides of the pulpit, each end being moved 12 feet and the space closed in, which provided room for 28 new pews. Over the following two years, the porch at the front entrance and the tower were built and the steeple added. During Captain Mowatt's bombardment in 1775, a cannonball went through the front wall and lodged inside, but the structure suffered no further damage.[*] The trial of Thomas Bird and Hans Hanson was held in this meeting house on June 5, 1790, because the courthouse was far too small to accommodate the curious crowds that had gathered to witness the event.

One block further east, on the site now occupied by Portland City Hall, the Cumberland County Court House, measuring 48 by 34 feet, was raised in 1785. Three years later the second floor containing the court room and offices was finished, and soon thereafter a cupola was added on which was mounted a carved weathercock. It has been suggested that St. Peter's predicted denials of Jesus Christ may have prompted the county elders to choose the symbol as a warning to all who entered that

_____

[*] When the stone building that is now the Unitarian-Universalist Church was built, the cannonball was used in the suspension of its glass chandelier.

within this temple of justice the truth must never be denied. Reminders were also purposefully placed on the first floor of the court house, which was an open hall where a gallows and stocks were stored in full view. And lest one fail to grasp the message, in front of the building they placed a whipping post in the shape of a cross. Federal District Judge David Sewall sentenced Thomas Bird to death in this court house on June 5, 1790.

Within two large areas bordered by Meetinghouse Lane (now Temple Street) on the west, Back Street on the north, The Lane (now Pearl Street) on the east, and Middle Street on the south, and divided by Lime Street, there was a swamp and two spring-fed ponds feeding brooks of considerable size that merged beyond Middle Street and ran under a stone bridge on Fore Street and into the harbor. Near the corner of Back and Pearl Streets a windmill rose above a small, rocky hill, probably built by Nathaniel Deering during the Revolution to mill corn, which previously had to be carried to Saccarappa Falls on the Presumpscot River in what is now Westbrook.

Greele's Tavern rested on the southeast corner of Back Street and Greele's Lane (now Hampshire Street). The tavern, a long, low, one-story house, was kept by Mrs. Alice Greele, a widow who was known far and wide for her irresistible baked beans. It was here that 33 delegates from the nine Cumberland County towns met on September 21, 1774, to debate several provocative acts of Parliament that took the authority to appoint civil officers from the people and vested it in the Crown. The delegation decided and publicly declared that no commissions bestowed by the Crown under these acts would be accepted or recognized.

Little more than a year later, when Captain Mowatt attacked the town, Mrs. Greele courageously remained in her home and saved it from destruction by extinguishing several fires. The court house in use at that time, however, did not survive the conflagration and, for the remainder of the war, court was held in a room rented from Mrs. Greele expressly for this purpose. This was also the site of a "jollification" held when news of Burgoyne's surrender reached Portland in October of 1777. The crowd drank with abandon as bottles of wine and buckets of punch were passed out of the tavern's windows, and a cannon was fired in celebration until a young man was mortally wounded by one of the balls. Benjamin Tukey,28, who had married Hannah Stanford less than two years earlier, was ramming a cartridge down the cannon's barrel when it prematurely discharged carrying away his right arm at the shoulder.

At the east end of Back Street, on the south side, the town's parade ground was laid out where Portland's militiamen marched in formation and practiced the manual of arms. Abutting this field on the harbor side was the burial ground resting in the shade of a lone and very tall Norway pine. Thomas Bird's body was laid to rest here in an unmarked grave. The area between the cemetery and the harbor was predominantly swamp land.

Munjoy Hill

At the foot of Munjoy Hill a stone wall stretched from Back Cove to the harbor with a gate at the end of Back Street that allowed access for the livestock that grazed on the hill. The town sold "cow rights", one being equal in value to about three acres of land. The hill also had a growth of trees and bushes at that time.

There were many in the town who remembered the conference held on the summit of Munjoy Hill in 1727 that ended Dummer's War during which the Massachusetts legislature placed a bounty on Indian scalps. In July of that year, more than 200 Indians representing the Arreguntonocks, Wawenocks, Norridgewocks, and Penobscots displaying the French flag gathered under a spacious tent to negotiate a peace with more than 40 delegates representing Maine and Massachusetts. A public dinner was provided at the expense of the government, but Rev. Dr. Thomas Smith wrote in his journal "they left us quite bare and nothing of the country's produce left, only three bushels of corn and some small things."[116]

More recent were memories of hundreds of tents blanketing the hill and campfires eerily lighting it through the night in August and September of 1779. Colonel Henry Jackson's regiment had been sent to repel a second British invasion of Portland that was anticipated but never came. [117]

∧∧∧∧

There were no banks in Portland in 1790, but there were, of course, many other shops, homes, and naked chimneys rising from charred timbers scattered along its streets at this time. Most of these belonged to individuals and families of little historical prominence, but of profound historical consequence.

They were of hardy stock. A century earlier many of their forebears had been killed or driven out during the French and Indian Wars. But these people of The Neck had returned, cleared the land, rebuilt their homes and replanted their gardens. Though many succumbed to brutal winters, meager rations, sickness, childbirth, stormy seas, and terrible accidents, most survived, and multiplied, and reclaimed the land.

BIBLIOGRAPHY

BIBLIOGRAPHY

BOOKS

Anderson, Joseph Crook II, ed., *Maine Families in 1790, Vol. 8, Maine Genealogical Society Special Publication No. 42*. Rockport, Maine: Picton Press, 2003.

Atlantic Navigator, The: Being a Nautical Description of the Coasts of France, Spain and Portugal, the West Coast of Africa, 4th ed. London: James Imray and Son, 1854.

Bailey, Sarah Loring. *Historical Sketches of Andover (Comprising the Present Towns of North Andover and Andover) Massachusetts*. Boston: Houghton, Mifflin and Company, 1880.

Bangs, Ella M. *An Historic Mansion: The Wadsworth-Longfellow House, Portland*. Portland, Maine: The Lamson Studio, 1903.

Boyle, James. M.C.S.L., Colonial Surgeon to Sierra Leone, Surgeon, R.N., *A Practical Medico-Historical Account of the Western Coast of Africa: Embracing a Topographical Description of its Shores, Rivers, and Settlements*. London: Oliver & Boyd, Edinburg; and Hodges & Smith, Dublin, 1831.

Dening, Greg. *Mr Bligh's Bad Language: Passion, Power and Theatre on the Bounty*. New York:

BIBLIOGRAPHY

Cambridge University Press, 1992.

Department of Commerce & Labor, Bureau of Census, S.N.D. North, Director. *Heads of Families at the First Census of the United States Taken in the Year 1790, Maine.* Wash DC: Government Printing Office, 1908

Dow, George Francis. *Slave Ships and Slaving.* Salem, MA: The Marine Research Society, 1927. Reprint, Mineola, NY: Dover Publications, 2002.

Elwell, Edward H. *The Successful Business Houses of Portland.* Portland, Maine: W.S. Jones, Publisher, 1875.

------. *Portland And Vicinity: With A Sketch Of Old Orchard Beach And Other Maine Resorts,* Rev. Ed. Portland, Maine: Loring, Short & Harmon, 1881.

------. *The Schools of Portland: From the Earliest Times to the Centennial Year of the Town, 1886.* Portland, Maine: William M. Marks, Printer, 1888.

Findlay, Alexander G. *A Sailing Directory for the Ethiopic or South Atlantic Ocean including the Coasts of South America and Africa,* 5th ed. London: Richard Holmes Laurie, 1867.

Freeman, Samuel. *Extracts from the Journals kept by the Rev. Thomas Smith, Late Pastor of the First Church of Christ in Falmouth, in the County of York, (Now Cumberland,) from the Year 1720, to the Year 1788, with an Appendix, containing a Variety of Other Matters.* Portland, Maine: Thomas Todd & Co., 1821.

Goold, Nathan. *Falmouth Neck in the Revolution.* Portland, Maine: Thurston Press, 1897.

------ . *A History of Peaks Island and its People, Also a Short Story of House Island, Portland, Maine.* Portland, Maine: Lakeside Press, 1897.

Goold, William. *Portland In The Past with Historical Notes of Old Falmouth.* Portland, Maine: B. Thurston & Co., 1886.

Hebert, Richard A. *Modern Maine: Its Historic Background, People and Resources,* Vol. II. New York: Lewis Historical Publishing Co., 1951.

Jones, Herbert G. *The King's Highway from Portland to Kittery: Stagecoach & Tavern Days on the Old Post Road.* Portland,

ME: The Longfellow Press, 1953.

Jordan, William B. Jr. *Burial Records 1717-1962 of the Eastern Cemetery Portland, Maine.* Bowie, MD: Heritage Books, 1987.

Little, George Thomas, ed., *Genealogical and Family History of the State of Maine,* Vol. II. New York: Lewis Historical Publ. Co., 1909.

McQueen, James. *A Geographical Survey of Africa, Its Rivers, Lakes, Mountains, Productions, States, Population.* London: B. Fellowes, 1840.

Nash, Charles Elventon. *The History of Augusta: First Settlements and Early Days as a Town Including the Diary of Mrs. Martha Moore Ballard (1785 to 1812).* Augusta, ME: Charles E. Nash & Son, 1904

North, James W. *The History of Augusta, Maine: A facsimile of the 1870 edition with a new foreword by Edwin A. Churchill.* Somersworth, NH: New England History Press, 1981.

Pickard, Samuel T. *Hawthorne's First Diary.* Boston: Houghton, Mifflin, 1897.

Purdy, John. *Memoir, Descriptive and Explanatory, to accompany the New Chart of the Ethiopic or Southern Atlantic Ocean.* London: R. H. Laurie, 1822.

Rawley, James A. *The Transatlantic Slave Trade: A History.* New York: W.W. Norton & Co., 1981.

Rediker, Marcus. *Between the Devil and the Deep Blue Sea: Merchant Seamen, Pirates and the Anglo-American Maritime World, 1700-1750.* Cambridge, U.K.: Cambridge University Press, 1987. Reprint, New York: Cambridge Univerity Press, 2004.

Shettleworth, Earle G. Jr., and William David Barry. *Mr. Goodhue Remembers Portland: Scenes from the Mid-19th Century.* Portland, Maine: Maine Historic Preservation Commission, 1981.

Shipton, Clifford K. *Sibley's Harvard Graduates Vol XIII 1751-1755: Biographical Sketches Of Those Who Attended Harvard College in the Classes 1751-1755 with Bibliographical and Other Notes.* Boston: Massachusetts Historical Society,

1965.

------. *Sibley's Harvard Graduates, Vol. XVII 1768-1771: Biographical Sketches of Those Who Attended Harvard College in the Classes 1667-1771 with Bibliographical and Other Notes.* Boston: Massachusetts Historical Society, 1975.

Smith, William H. *"General Henry Dearborn. A Genealogical Sketch"* Vol. III of The Maine Historical and Genealogical Recorder. Portland, Maine: S.M. Watson, Publ., 1886.

Spencer, Wilbur D. *Maine Immortals: Including Many Unique Characters in Early Maine History.* Augusta, ME: Northeastern Press, 1932.

Willis, William. *Journals of the Rev. Thomas Smith, and the Rev. Samuel Deane, Pastors of the First Church in Portland: With Notes and Biographical Notices: And a Summary History of Portland.* Portland, Maine: Joseph S. Bailey, 1849.

------. *A History of The Law, The Courts, and The Lawyers of Maine, from its First Colonization to the Early Part of the Present Century.* Portland, Maine: Bailey & Noyes, 1863.

------, *The History of Portland, 2 vols.* (1831, 1833); A facsimile of the second edition published in 1865 in one volume with a new foreword by Gerald Morris. Portland, Maine: Maine Historical Society, 1972.

Yerxa, Donald A. *The Burning of Falmouth, 1775. A Case Study in British Imperial Pacification.* Portland, Maine: Maine Historical Society, 1975.

UNPUBLISHED DOCUMENTS

National Archives, Waltham, MA. H. Sewall, Clerk, *U.S. District Court at Portland, June Term, 1790.*

------. Charles Cushing, Clerk, *Precept Issued by the Supreme Judicial Court, Cumberland South, Commonwealth of Massachusetts,* 23 July 1789.

------. *Examination of Hans Hanson before the Supreme Judicial Court, Cumberland South, Commonwealth of Massachusetts,"* 23 July 1789.

------. *Examination of Mathias* (Josiah) *Jackson before the Supreme Judicial Court, Cumberland South, Commonwealth of Massachusetts,"* 23 July 1789.

------. *"Examination of Thomas Bird before the Supreme Judicial Court, Cumberland South, Commonwealth of Massachusetts,"* 24 July 1789.

------. *"Invoice of Sundry Goods found on board a Sloop (taken by Cap't Barker & others) supposed to be piratically bro.'t from the Coast of Africa by Jackson & others, now in Custody, John Waite, Sheriff,"* 27 July 1789.

------. *Jurors for trial of the Criminals Thomas Bird & Hans Hanson.*

------. H. Sewall, Clerk, *The United States prosecutors vs Thomas Bird late resident of Bristol in the Kingdom of Great Britain.* June 5, 1790.

------. John Waite, Sheriff, (*L)ist of names of Persons who had rec^d goods out of the Sloop Mary lately brought into this Port by Capt. John Baker and others previous to his taking possession of her and have not returned the same agreeable to the order of Court.*

WEBSITES

"America's Historical Newspapers including Early American Newspapers Series 1, 1690-1876", Readex, *http://infoweb.newsbank.com/iw-search/we/HistArchive* (accessed March 1, 2009).

"The History of the First Parish in Portland, Maine, Old Jerusalem 1740-1825". The First Parish in Portland, Maine,

BIBLIOGRAPHY

Unitarian-Universalist,
http://www.firstparishportland.org/history3.html
(accessed May 9, 2009).

"HMS Bounty." Wikipedia, The free encyclopedia,
http://en.wikipedia.org/wiki/HMS_Bombay
(accessed August 28, 2008).

"The Mutiny on HMS Bounty". Royal Naval Museum, Research.
http://www.royalnavalmuseum.org/
Info_sheets_bounty.htm
(accessed August 28, 2008).

"New Hampshire Almanac ". A Brief History of New Hampshire,
http://www.nh.gov/nhinfo/history.html
(accessed April 20, 2009).

"Thomas Bird to George Washington (June 5, 1790)." The
Papers of George Washington: Presidential Series, 5. The
Constitutional Sources Project http://www.consource.
org/index.asp?bid=582&fid=600&documented=58425
(accessed May 9, 2009).

"To Judge David Sewall." The writings of George Washington
from the original manuscript sources Electronic Text Center,
University of Virginia Library.
http://etext.virginia.edu/etcbin/toccer-new2?id=WasFi31.
Xml&images=images/modeng&data=/texts/English/modeng
/parsed&tag=public&part=64&division-div1
(accessed October 25, 2008).

"U.S. Constitution: Eighth Amendment, Excessive Bail", FindLaw
For Legal Professionals http://caselaw.lp.findlaw.com/
data/constitution/amendment08/01.html
(accessed September 10, 2008).

NEWSPAPERS

"Billy and Harry Hans", Portland (Maine) Daily Eastern
Argus, Vol. 13, p. 7, 23 November 1912.

"Hawthorne", The New York Times, 7 June 1902.

PORTLAND NECK

"Portland," Portland (Maine) Cumberland Gazette, 31 July 1789, 7 June 1790, 28 June 1790.

"Salaries", Portland (Maine) Cumberland Gazette, 1 March 1790.

END NOTES

END NOTES

I - THOMAS BIRD

[1] Marcus Rediker, *Between the Devil and the Deep Blue Sea: Merchant Seamen, Pirates and the Anglo-American Maritime World, 1700-1750* (Cambridge, U.K.: Cambridge University Press, 1987. Reprint, New York: Cambridge Univerity Press, 2004), 42.

[2] "HMS Bounty." Wikipedia, The free encyclopedia, http://en.wikipedia.org/wiki/HMS_Bombay (accessed August 28, 2008).

[3] "The Mutiny on HMS Bounty". Research. Royal Naval Museum, http://www.royalnavalmuseum.org/ info_sheets_bounty.htm (accessed August 28, 2008).

[4] Greg Dening, *Mr Bligh's Bad Language: Passion, Power and Theatre on the Bounty* (New York: Cambridge University Press, 1992), 19.

[5] Ibid., 36.

[6] "Portland," Portland (Maine) Cumberland Gazette, 31 July 1789.

[7] Ibid.

[8] Rediker, *Devil and the Deep Blue Sea*, 31.

[9] Ibid., 29.

[10] *"Examination of Thomas Bird before the Supreme Judicial Court, Cumberland South, Commonwealth of Massachusetts,"* 24 July 1789. Record held at the National Archives, Waltham, MA.

[11] *"Examination of Thomas Bird, op. cit."* and *Examination of Hans Hanson before the Supreme Judicial Court, Cumberland South, Commonwealth of Massachusetts,"* 23 July 1789. Record held at the National Archives, Waltham, MA.

[12] Rediker, *Devil and the Deep Blue Sea*, 85.

[13] Ibid., 46.

[14] George Francis Dow, *Slave Ships and Slaving* (Salem, MA: The Marine Research Society, 1927. Reprint, Mineola, NY: Dover Publications, 2002), 175.

[15] James A. Rawley, *The Transatlantic Slave Trade: A History* (New York: W.W. Norton & Co., 1981), p. 285

[16] Rediker, *Devil and the Deep Blue Sea*, 81-82.

[17] *"Examination of Thomas Bird, op. cit."*

[18] *"Invoice of Sundry Goods found on board a Sloop (taken by Cap't Barker & others) supposed to be piratically bro.'t from the Coast of Africa by Jackson & others, now in Custody, John Waite, Sheriff,"* 27 July 1789. Record held at the National Archives, Waltham, MA.

II - THE GUINEA COAST

[19] Dow, *Slave Ships and Slaving*, 12.

[20] Ibid., 62-63.

[21] James Boyle, M.C.S.L., Colonial Surgeon to Sierra Leone, Surgeon, R.N., *A Practical Medico-Historical Acount of the Western Coast of Africa: Embracing a Topographical Description of its Shores, Rivers, and Settlements . . . .* (London: Oliver & Boyd, Edinburg; and Hodges & Smith, Dublin, 1831), 308.

[22] *The Atlantic Navigator: Being a Nautical Description of the Coasts of France, Spain and Portugal, the West Coast of Africa . . . ,* 4th ed. (London: James Imray and Son, 1854), 151.

[23] Alexander G. Findlay, Fellow of the Royal Geographical Society, *A Sailing Directory for the Ethiopic or South Atlantic Ocean including the Coasts of South America and Africa,* 5th ed. (London: Richard Holmes Laurie, 1867), 471.

[24] Dow, *Slave Ships and Slaving*, 2-5.

[25] James McQueen, Esq., *A Geographical Survey of Africa, Its Rivers, Lakes, Mountains, Productions, States, Population . . . .* (London: B. Fellowes, 1840), 26-27.

[26] *"Examination of Hans Hanson, op. cit."*

[27] Findlay, *A Sailing Directory for the Ethiopic or South Atlantic Ocean,* 456.

[28] Ibid., 463.

[29] John Purdy, Hydrographer, *Memoir, Descriptive and Explanatory, to accompany the New Chart of the Ethiopic or Southern Atlantic Ocean . . . .* (London: R. H. Laurie, 1822), 74.

[30] Findlay, *A Sailing Directory for the Ethiopic or South Atlantic Ocean,* 464.

[31] *Examination of Mathias* (Josiah) *Jackson before the Supreme Judicial Court, Cumberland South, Commonwealth of Massachusetts,"* 23 July 1789. Record held at the National Archives, Waltham, MA.

[32] Findlay, *A Sailing Directory for the Ethiopic or South Atlantic Ocean,* 473.

[33] Ibid., 479.

[34] Boyle, *A Practical Medico-Historical Account of the Western Coast of Africa,* 324-28.

[35] Ibid., 328.

[36] *"Examination of Hans Hanson, op. cit."*

[37] Purdy, *Memoir, Descriptive and Explanatory, to accompany the New Chart . . . ,* 76.

III – THE MIDDLE PASSAGE AND CAPTURE

[38] Findlay, *Sailing Directory for the Ethiopic or South Atlantic Ocean,* 478.

[39] Boyle, *Practical Medico-Historical Account of the Western Coast of Africa,* 332-33.

[40] *The Atlantic Navigator,* 180.

[41] John Waite, Sheriff, *(L)ist of names of Persons who had rec^d goods out of the Sloop Mary lately brought into this Port by Capt. John Baker and others previous to his taking possession of her and have not returned the same agreeable to the order of Court.* Record held at the National Archives, Waltham, MA.

[42] William Willis, *The History of Portland,* 2 vols. (1831, 1833); Facsimile of the second edition published in 1865 in one volume with a new foreword by Gerald Morris, Portland, Maine: Maine Historical Society, 1972), 462.

[43] *"Portland,"* Cumberland Gazette (Portland, Maine), 31 July 1789.

[44] Charles Cushing, Clerk, *Precept Issued by the Supreme Judicial Court, Cumberland South, Commonwealth of Massachusetts,* 23 July 1789. Record held at the National Archives, Waltham, MA.

[45] *Examination of Hans Hanson, op. cit.*

[46] *Examination of Mathias (Josiah) Jackson,* op. cit.

[47] *York County Register of Deeds,* Book 50, Page 23.

[48] "U.S. Constitution: Eighth Amendment, Excessive Bail", FindLaw For Legal Professionals http://caselaw.lp.findlaw.com/ data/constitution/ amendment08/01.html , (accessed September 10, 2008).

[49] Samuel Freeman, Esq., *Extracts from the Journals kept by the Rev. Thomas Smith, Late Pastor of the First Church of Christ in Falmouth, in the County of York, (Now Cumberland,) from the Year 1720, to the Year 1788, with an Appendix, containing a Variety of Other Matters* (Portland, Maine: Thomas Todd & Co., 1821), 65.

[50] *Examination of Thomas Bird,* op. cit.

[51] John Waite, Sheriff, *Invoice of Sundry Goods found on board a Sloop (taken by Capt Baker & others) supposed to be piratically bro^t from the Coast of Africa by Jackson & others, now in Custody,* 27 July 1789. Record held at the National Archives, Waltham, MA.

[52] Waite, *(L)ist of names of Persons,* op.cit.

[53] William Goold, *Portland In The Past With Historical Notes of Old Falmouth* (1886; reprint, Bowie, Maryland: Heritage Books, Inc., 1997), 496.

[54] Freeman, *Extracts from the Journals,* 64-65.

[55] *Collections and Proceedings of the Maine Historical Society, Second Series,* Vol. II (Portland, Maine: Maine Historical Society, 1891), 303.

[56] Clifford K. Shipton, *Sibley's Harvard Graduates, Vol. XIII – 1751-1755, Biographical Sketches of Those Who Attended Harvard College in the classes 1751-1755 with Bibliographical and Other Notes,* (Boston: Massachusetts Historical Society, 1965), 642.

[57] *Collections and Proceedings of the Maine Historical Society,* Second Series, Vol. II (Portland, ME: Maine Historical Society, 1891), 301-02.

[58] William Willis, *A History of the Law, the Courts, and the Lawyers of Maine, from its First Colonization to the Early Part of the Present Century* (Portland, Maine: Bailey & Noyes, 1863), 86.

[59] George Thomas Little, A.M., Litt. D., ed., *Genealogical and Family History of the State of Maine,* Vol. II (New York: Lewis Historical Publ. Co., 1909), 771-72.

[60] James W. North, *The History of Augusta, Maine: A facsimile of the 1870 edition with a new foreword by Edwin A. Churchill* (Somersworth, NH: New England History Press, 1981), 224-25.

[61] Ibid., 226-28.

[62] Freeman, *Extracts from the Journals,* 65.

IV – THE TRIAL

[63] Goold, Portland in the Past, 496.

[64] Willis, History of Portland, 823.

[65] Goold, Portland in the Past, 500-01.

[66] Goold, Portland in the Past, 498-99.

[67] Ibid., 370.

[68] H. Sewall, Clerk, *U.S. District Court at Portland, June Term, 1790.* Record held at the National Archives, Waltham, MA.

[69] Ibid.

[70] Richard A. Hebert, *Modern Maine: Its Historic Background, People and Resources,* Vol. II, (New York: Lewis Historical Publishing Co., 1951), 47.

[71] Freeman, Extracts of the Journal of Rev. Thomas Smith, 65.

[72] *Jurors for trial of the Criminals Thomas Bird & Hans Hanson.* Record held at the National Archives, Waltham, MA.

[73] Freeman, Extracts, 65.

[74] "Portland", Cumberland Gazette (Portland, Maine), 7 June 1790.

[75] Freeman, Extracts, 65.

[76] H. Sewall, Clerk, *The United States prosecutors vs Thomas Bird late resident of Bristol in the Kingdom of Great Britain.* June 5, 1790. Record held at the National Archives, Waltham, MA.

[77] "Sentence of Death", Cumberland Gazette (Portland, Maine), 7 June 1790.

[78] "Thomas Bird to George Washington (June 5, 1790)." The Papers of George Washington: Presidential Series, 5. The Constitutional Sources Project. http://www.consource.org/index.asp?bid=582&fid=600&documentid=58425 (accessed May 9, 2009).

[79] Goold, Portland in the Past, 501.

END NOTES

80 "To Judge David Sewall." *The writings of George Washington from the original manuscript sources* Electronic Text Center, University of Virginia Library. http://etext.virginia.edu/etcbin/toccer-new2?id=WasFi31.xml&images=images/modeng&data=/texts/english/modeng/parsed&tag=public&part=64&division=div1 (accessed October 25, 2008).

V – THE EXECUTION

81 William Willis, *Journals of the Rev. Thomas Smith, and the Rev. Samuel Deane, Pastors of the First Church in Portland: With Notes and Biographical Notices: And a Summary History of Portland* (Portland, Maine: Joseph S. Bailey, 1849), 358.

82 Goold, Portland in the Past, 500-01.

83 Department of Commerce & Labor, Bureau of Census, S.N.D. North, Director, *Heads of Families at the First Census of the United States Taken in the Year 1790, Maine,* (Wash DC: Government Printing Office, 1908), 9.

84 "Portland", Portland (Maine) Cumberland Gazette, 28 June 1790.

85 William B. Jordan, Jr., *Burial Records 1717-1962 of the Eastern Cemetery Portland, Maine* (Bowie, MD: Heritage Books, 1987), 10.

86 "America's Historical Newspapers including Early American Newspapers Series 1, 1690-1876", Readex, http://infoweb.newsbank.com/iw-search/we/HistArchive (Accessed March 1, 2009).

PORTLAND, MAINE 1789-90

87 Now Cushing Island and Cape Elizabeth.

88 Willis, *The History of Portland,* 581.

89 Ibid, 570.

90 Ibid, 111.

91 Ibid, 108.

92 Ibid, 583.

[93] Edward H. Elwell, *Portland And Vicinity: With A Sketch Of Old Orchard Beach And Other Maine Resorts,* Rev. Ed. (Portland, Maine: Loring, Short & Harmon, 1881), 51.

[94] *Heads of Families at the First Census of the United States Taken in the Year 1790, Maine,* Dept. of Commerce & Labor, Bureau of Census, S.N.D. North, Director (Wash DC: Government Printing Office, 1908), 9.

[95] "New Hampshire Almanac", A Brief History of New Hampshire, http://www.nh.gov/nhinfo/history.html (accessed April 20, 2009).

[96] Willis, The History of Portland, 324-26.

[97] Edward H. Elwell, *The Successful Business Houses of Portland* (Portland, Maine: W.S. Jones, Publisher, 1875), 186.

[98] Edward H. Elwell, *The Schools of Portland: From the Earliest Times to the Centennial Year of the Town, 1886* (Portland, Maine: William M. Marks, Printer, 1888), 7-8

[99] Willis, *The History of Portland,* 360.

[100] Ibid, 399.

[101] Ibid, 398-402.

[102] Ibid, 647.

[103] Ibid, 407.

[104] Herbert G. Jones, *The King's Highway from Portland to Kittery: Stagecoach & Tavern Days on the Old Post Road* (Portland, ME: The Longfellow Press, 1953), 20-22.

[105] Ibid, 23-24.

[106] William Goold, *Portland in the Past with Historical Notes of Old Falmouth,* (Portland, Maine: B. Thurston & Co., 1886), 500-01.

[107] Elwell, *Successful Business Houses of Portland,* 180.

[108] Donald A. Yerxa, *The Burning of Falmouth, 1775. A Case Study in British Imperial Pacification,* (Portland, Maine: Maine Historical Society, 1975), 140-41.

[109] Willis, *The History of Portland,* 521 fn.

[110] Elwell, *Successful Business Houses of Portland,* 185.

[111] Earle G. Shettleworth, Jr., and William David Barry, *Mr. Goodhue Remembers Portland: Scenes from the Mid-19th Century,* (Portland, Maine: Maine Historic Preservation Commission, 1981), (20).

[112] Goold, *Portland in the Past,* 495-96.

[113] "Billy and Harry Hans", Daily Eastern Argus, Vol. 13, Nov. 23, 1912, 7.

[114] Ella M. Bangs, *An Historic Mansion: The Wadsworth-Longfellow House, Portland,* (Portland, Maine: The Lamson Studio, 1903, 6-7.

[115] "The History of the First Parish in Portland, Maine, Old Jerusalem 1740-1825", The First Parish in Portland, Maine, Unitarian-Universalist, http://www.firstparishportland.org/history3.html (accessed on May 9, 2009).

[116] Willis, *History of Portland,* 352.

[117] Goold, Nathan, *Falmouth Neck in the Revolution,* (Portland, Maine: Thurston Press, 1897), 46.